Book 8

Using Christian Decks as Your First "Mutual Success Project"

Hundreds of Ways to Share God's Word—and Earn from It

By Mr. Elijah J Stone
and the Team Success Network

Using Christian Decks as Your First "Mutual Success Project"

Team Success Network Publishing
Email: connect@teamsuccessnetwork.com

Published by Team Success Network Publishing
Printed in the United States of America

ISBN (Paperback): 978-1-968654-07-8
Library of Congress Control Number: 2025913892
First Edition: June 2025

Cover Design by: Team Success Creative
Interior Layout by: Team Success Creative

Contact Us – Let's Build Together

This is more than a book. It's an invitation. A call to rise, to act, to build—together.

The "Team Success Network" exists to support churches, ministries, and Christian groups as they pursue God's vision: bringing Heaven to Earth through unified, purpose-driven action. If this message stirs something in you, or if you're ready to explore what mutual success looks like in your community—we want to hear from you.

Let's start the conversation.

Reach out here:

📩 General Connection – connect@teamsuccessnetwork.com

📩 Share Your Team's Results & Testimonies – results@teamsuccessnetwork.com

📩 Submit Documents or Project Materials – docs@teamsuccessnetwork.com

📩 Contact Elijah Personally – elijah@teamsuccessnetwork.com

We're here to support, encourage, and collaborate. Whether you're just starting out or leading a growing movement—this is your first step. Let's build something eternal.

Table of Contents

Preface: "Inquire on the Lord" For Success In Everything – Especially This 9

PART 1: The Opportunity 15

CHAPTER 1: What is a Scripture Deck and why it's powerful 16

CHAPTER 2: Testimony Origin Story - Of How Christian Decks Started .. 23

CHAPTER 3: "God Reminders" - How Scripture Cards Can Bring the Kingdom of Heaven to the Earth 30

CHAPTER 4: "The Call of God" - Why This Is More Than a Business - It's a Mission 37

CHAPTER 5: The Origin of "Team Success" & the "Mutual Success Team" 44

CHAPTER 6: "Mutual Success Team" - Your First Project - Earn while spreading the Word - in a way that fits you perfectly 52

CHAPTER 7: What Makes This & You Different? "Mutual Success" is a New Powerful Idea 59

CHAPTER 8: Being Willing to Mentor Others & Share Everything 67

CHAPTER 9: Why You Should Succeed - Part 1 - 7 Reasons Why - What's Stacked In Your Favor? 74

CHAPTER 10: Why You Should Succeed - Part 2 - "The Mutual Success Solution": What's Stacked In Your Favor? 82

PART 2: The Stories – The Path Ahead: What Your Success Story Could Look Like 90

CHAPTER 11: "The Stories": Inspiring You & Showing You The Potential 91

CHAPTER 12: "The Stories" - The Mom At Home 96

CHAPTER 13: "The Stories" - The Youth Group Leader 101

CHAPTER 14: "The Stories" - The Retired Couple At a Farmer's Market 106
CHAPTER 15: "The Stories" - The College Student Online 111
CHAPTER 16: "The Stories" - The Pastor Funding Their Next Project ...116
CHAPTER 17: The entrepreneur building recurring cash flow 121

PART 3: The Deck – Card Business System Explained 127
CHAPTER 18: How the Cards Work: Scripture + relationship building..128
CHAPTER 19: The Pricing Strategy: Why $20 works perfectly 133
CHAPTER 20: The Target Market: Who buys (everyone needs encouragement) 140
CHAPTER 21: The Selling Process: Natural, relationship-based approach 147
CHAPTER 22: The Profit Structure: How everyone wins 153
CHAPTER 23: Introducing - The "Mutual Success Team" Deck - How It Was Designed 160

PART 4: The Deck – Cards Showcase 167
CHAPTER 24: The Card Showcase - Showing all 54 Cards 168

PART 5: The Tools – What You Need To Succeed 183
CHAPTER 25: Choosing Your Method - Part 1 184
CHAPTER 26: Choosing Your Method - Part 2 191
CHAPTER 27: Getting Started Fast - Part 1 199
CHAPTER 28: Getting Started Fast - Part 2 206
CHAPTER 29: Scaling Your Success - Part 1 213
CHAPTER 30: Scaling Your Success - Part 2 221
CHAPTER 31: Building Your Community - Part 1 229
CHAPTER 32: Building Your Community - Part 2 236

PART 6: The Templates – For Leading Your Team 244
CHAPTER 33: Weekly Meeting Agenda (provided template)................245
CHAPTER 34: Monthly Goal Setting (provided worksheets) 253
CHAPTER 35: Quarterly Celebrations (provided event plans)...............262
CHAPTER 36: Annual Vision Renewal (provided retreat guide)............273

Part 7: The Ways – Finally Pick Your Favorite Way To Sell From 100+ 283
CHAPTER 37: Try Your Favorite Idea for 30 Days / Experiment For a Month 284
CHAPTER 38: "To Our Mutual Success" Together................................292

CHAPTER 39: The 100+ Ways You Can Sell Christian Decks – Start Picking Your Favorite...298

Preface: "Inquire on the Lord" For Success In Everything – Especially This

Let the Good Shepherd Lead You Into Results

We Begin With God—Because Success Begins With Direction

Every lasting success begins at the same place: with the Lord. Before you form your team, before you launch a business idea, and before you set goals—pause and ask. Ask who? Ask Him. The One who already sees your future, your finances, your calling, and your purpose. If you're holding this book, it's not just a business decision—it's an invitation to walk with God in building something that matters.

If you're looking for breakthrough—whether in purpose, income, or impact—there's one habit more powerful than any technique: learning to inquire of the Lord. Not in a religious way. Not in a superstitious way. But in a relational way. Inquiring means asking for guidance. It's your way of saying, "I don't want to do this without You."

And if you do that... your path becomes clear.

Inquire First—Then Build Boldly

Scripture says, *"If we ask anything according to His will, He hears us... and we know we have what we asked"* (1 John 5:14–15). That's not wishful thinking—it's strategy. It means that alignment with God *precedes* acceleration in results. Your success isn't just about energy or hustle—it's about direction. And only God can give you the exact direction that leads to the breakthrough you're truly seeking.

Before launching into this project—or any project—ask:

- **"Lord, is this the right Mutual Success Project for me?"**
- **"How do You want me to start?"**

Those two questions can define your path. They bring clarity where there was confusion. They invite God into the driver's seat, where He belongs.

Why This Project? Why Now?

This Christian Decks opportunity is more than a small product—it's a **Mutual Success Project** that could change your financial future. It's the first project we recommend for new Team Success members because:

- It's simple to start
- It's easy to explain
- It's deeply meaningful
- And it works

But even more than that—it's something you can pray about, inquire about, and receive direction about. If it's right for you, God will make it clear. If there's another path, He'll show you that too. He's not hiding the answer.

So don't guess. Ask.

He Leads—We Follow

Jesus described Himself not as a consultant or a coach—but as a **Shepherd**. He said, *"My sheep hear My voice... and they follow Me"* (John 10:27). That's a powerful picture. It tells us that the Christian life—and Christian business—is not meant to be lived in independence. It's meant to be led.

This means your best results come when you're not just charging ahead... but listening first.

David, one of the greatest leaders in the Bible, never assumed. He *inquired of the Lord*—again and again. He asked before every battle. He didn't rely on past victories. And because he asked, he won. His strength wasn't in his sword—it was in his surrender.

You can have that same strength. It begins with a question: "God, what are You doing—and how do I partner with it?"

Practical Direction—Starts With Pausing

What if your next breakthrough idea doesn't come from brainstorming—but from listening?

Many people rush into business or ministry with their own plans, and they ask God to bless it afterward. But what if we flipped that? What if we inquired *first*, and built *second*? What if we paused long enough to hear what He already wants to do—and then moved with confidence in that direction?

That's not superstition. That's strategy.

When you hear from the Lord first, your steps are stable. Your words are bold. Your marketing becomes authentic. You're not hoping for success—you're moving with divine momentum.

Here's a Simple Way to Start

Try this:

- Set aside 10 minutes in the morning.
- Ask: *"Lord, is this the project for me?"*
- Ask: *"How do You want me to begin?"*
- Listen. Wait. Write down what comes.

You may hear an idea. You may see a picture. You may just feel a gentle pull in one direction. Whatever it is—acknowledge it. Follow it. Don't overthink it. Let that quiet response become your guide for the day.

And if nothing comes, don't worry. Try again tomorrow. The habit of asking *matters as much* as the answer.

Two Keys to Inquire About

As you start this journey, come back to these two key questions again and again:

1. **Is this the right "Mutual Success Project" for me right now?**
   God may confirm it through peace, inspiration, or a repeated nudge. He may highlight your strengths and say: "You're ready for this."
2. **What is my next step with this project?**
   You don't need to know the whole plan. Just ask for the next action. It could be reaching out to one person. Designing your

first deck. Watching a quick training. You don't have to climb the mountain in a day—you just have to take the first step in the right direction.

Your First Mutual Success Team Project—Built With God

This project is meant to bless you. It's built around **team collaboration**, **low pressure**, and **real income potential**. But don't let simplicity fool you—this is a tool God can use to answer your prayers. It can be your starting point for financial peace, ministry impact, and long-term overflow.

But it works best when you make it **relational**—not just **transactional**. That's why we begin by saying: **Inquire of the Lord**.

Let Him guide your thinking.

Let Him bless your hands.

Let Him lead your team.

Breakthrough Comes Through Alignment

There's no shortage of business ideas in the world. But this is different. It's rooted in Scripture. It's built for community. It's meant to create spiritual and financial abundance at the same time.

But even this project—if done without God—can fall flat. So choose the better way. Inquire.

Ask before you post. Ask before you launch. Ask before you plan your month. Don't just act—align.

When you align with Him, the results take care of themselves.

Ask. Inquire. Listen. Follow.

That's the rhythm of success in the Kingdom. And that's how your journey with Mutual Success Projects should begin.

You're not in this alone. You're building something with God. He cares about your income. He cares about your impact. And He wants to show you the way.

So today—before you start anything else—pause and ask:
"Lord, is this the path You have for me?"
"What do You want to do through me here?"

Then follow. Boldly. Faithfully. Joyfully.

This is the way to real results. This is the way to Mutual Success.

Part 1: The Opportunity

What if one small deck of cards could change the way you share God's Word—and how you earn a living? In this part, we introduce you to the quiet power of Scripture Decks and how they're becoming the first successful "Mutual Success Project" for Christians everywhere.

You'll discover how something so small—just 52 verses—can become a powerful spiritual tool, a business opportunity, and a daily devotional all in one. We'll walk through how Christian Decks began, what inspired it, and how you can use it to bring more of Heaven into your everyday life.

This isn't just another business idea. It's a Kingdom mission. When you begin to view your work, your earnings, and your daily habits as acts of discipleship—everything changes. You'll see why "Team Success" and "Mutual Success Teams" matter now more than ever.

By the end of this section, you'll have a strong foundation. You'll understand why you were chosen for this. And why now is the perfect time to launch your first Mutual Success Project with something that brings life to others and income to you.

Chapter 1 – What Is a Scripture Deck and Why It's Powerful

The Word of God in your pocket, your hand, and your heart

Small Things Can Be Extremely Valuable

In the Kingdom of God, it's often the smallest things that carry the greatest power. Jesus taught that the mustard seed, although the tiniest of all seeds, becomes a massive tree—big enough to give shelter to the birds of the air. That image is not just poetic; it's deeply strategic. It tells us that small beginnings should never be underestimated.

The entire Gospel starts with a baby in a manger. The entire world was saved by a three-year ministry. And faith the size of a mustard seed? Jesus said it can move mountains. We live in a spiritual reality where little things—when filled with God—can produce explosive, eternal results.

That's the foundational truth behind the Scripture Deck. At first glance, it's just a deck of cards. But what if it was more than that?

What if something as small as a single verse, printed on a playing card, could anchor someone's day, comfort a hurting heart, or redirect the course of a person's life? That's exactly what these cards are built to do.

In a world overflowing with noise and complexity, the simplicity of a Scripture Deck becomes its secret weapon. It's small. It's focused. And because of that, it's powerful.

What Is a Scripture Deck?

A Scripture Deck is a set of 52 high-quality cards—each one carrying a powerful verse from the Bible. Styled like a traditional deck of playing cards, each one is easy to carry, fun to use, and spiritually meaningful. It's God's Word made mobile. Made visible. Made shareable.

At its core, this is a devotional tool disguised as a conversation piece. It's something you can keep by your bedside, on your kitchen table, or tucked in your backpack or purse. Pull one out each morning for encouragement. Gift one to a friend in need. Use it during small groups, mealtimes, youth meetings, or even game nights. It's the Word of God made active—placed into daily rhythms of life.

These decks aren't designed to replace the Bible. They're designed to keep it close. To help you remember it. Meditate on it. Share it. It's a way to carry the Word with you—not just digitally on an app, but physically, in your hands and in your environment.

The idea is simple, and that's the beauty. When you need a quick reminder of God's promises, a Scripture Deck gives you exactly what you need—without needing to flip through chapters or search online. Just pull a card. Read it. Let it speak.

Why It's More Effective Than Most Devotionals

Let's be honest—most devotionals are started with good intentions but rarely finished. People get busy. Chapters pile up. Guilt sets in. Eventually the book collects dust, and the connection to God's Word gets delayed another day.

Scripture Decks solve that problem. They remove guilt from the equation and make engagement effortless. There's no page number to keep up with. No pressure to finish. You just pick a card. Any card. And receive from God in that moment. You don't fall behind—you just pick back up.

And unlike traditional devotionals, Scripture Decks fit into your flow. They're not another thing to schedule. They meet you in the middle of your life. Over coffee. In a car ride. At a lunch break. With your family at dinner. They are flexible, portable, and immediately impactful.

They also create moments of sharing. You don't need to explain a theology or teach a sermon. You can just say, "Here, I thought of you," and hand someone a card. That scripture becomes a seed planted in their spirit—something they can carry, read again later, and be encouraged by long after the moment has passed.

It's personal, but not pressure-filled. It's deep, but not complicated. And that's what makes it work.

A Devotional, A Business, and A Ministry—All in One

The impact of a Scripture Deck goes far beyond the individual. When you start using one regularly, you begin to realize—this is a tool that can change households. Change routines. Change families. And yes, even build businesses.

Because people don't just need encouragement—they're looking for meaningful ways to engage others. Christian parents want something for their kids that's fun *and* biblical. Church leaders want discipleship tools that are simple, affordable, and versatile. Young believers want faith-based products they can actually share with their friends without being awkward.

And this one product—this one little deck of cards—meets all of those needs. Which is why it also becomes a business opportunity.

You don't need to "sell" a Scripture Deck. You just need to share it. Let people touch it, read it, and experience it. When they do, they get it. It clicks. And they often want one for themselves—or for someone they love. That's why these decks don't just spread the Word—they create a flow of Kingdom-based income for those who carry them forward.

This isn't just a devotional tool. It's a discipleship tool. A ministry tool. A relationship tool. A success tool. And for many, it becomes the very first business they ever launch, rooted in something eternal.

The Spiritual Strategy Hidden in the Cards

Behind the simplicity of a Scripture Deck lies a divine strategy. The Bible says, "Faith comes by hearing, and hearing by the Word of God." But faith also comes by repetition. By keeping the Word visible. By putting it before your eyes day and night.

That's what these cards do. They're subtle, but consistent. They create micro-moments of meditation. They reprogram your inner dialogue. They help you live by truth, not emotion.

They also work spiritually—because the Word of God is living and active. It changes things. It cuts through confusion. It brings clarity. When you hold a card in your hand, you're holding a spiritual sword. A promise. A weapon against fear, doubt, discouragement, and distraction.

And when you gather others around the same deck? Now you're building community. You're discipling without needing to prepare a sermon. You're leading with joy. You're multiplying faith in others. And you're doing it with a tool that requires zero credentials—just love and willingness.

That's why Scripture Decks are so much more than cards. They're containers of truth, catalysts for growth, and conversation starters for revival.

It Started Small, Like Every God-Thing Does

This whole project began with one man, in one house, with one idea—during one of the hardest seasons of his life. He wasn't trying to launch a business. He was trying to hold on to God. And in the middle of spiritual warfare, mental exhaustion, and total life collapse, he needed a way to stay grounded in the truth.

He needed reminders. Daily. Tangible. Visual. Verses that would anchor him in identity, hope, and faith. And one day, he remembered a set of playing cards from his past—used for productivity in a business setting. The idea hit: *What if these cards carried scripture instead?*

He sketched it out. He used ChatGPT to help develop the themes and verses. He designed the layout. He created his first deck. Not for others—but for himself. And as he used it, his focus shifted. His hope returned. His connection with God deepened.

Soon, others asked about it. Family. Friends. A few people at church. And slowly, a personal tool became a shared resource. A shared resource became a product. A product became a project.

And that project became the very first *Mutual Success Team* business model—one that you can now step into for yourself.

What Comes Next

In the next chapter, you'll hear that founder's full story. Not to glorify his past—but to show you how powerfully God can use the lowest point in someone's life to plant the seed of a Kingdom business.

You'll see that the idea of Christian Decks wasn't born from profit—it was born from pain. From prayer. From personal need. And because of that, it carries a deep authenticity and spiritual weight.

This isn't hype. It's hope. And it's available to you.

So keep reading. Something small could be about to grow big.

Chapter 2 – Testimony Origin Story: How Christian Decks Started

A spark in the dark. A quiet miracle in the middle of a storm.

When Everything in Life Blows Up

The story behind Christian Decks didn't begin in a place of strength or success. It began in a spiritual fog—a personal darkness that lasted over a decade. For more than 11 years, the founder of Christian Decks fought through what can only be described as a full-life takeover. Not just stress. Not just confusion. But a deep, extended battle of spiritual warfare that left him immobilized. It was the kind of struggle where you're not just lost—you don't even know what direction hope might be in.

He wasn't lazy. He wasn't bitter. He was trapped. For years, he couldn't function. Couldn't be relied on. Couldn't build or hold a job. And behind all of it was a storm so heavy that it felt supernatural—because it was. It wasn't just emotional exhaustion. It was spiritual warfare of the highest order.

But here's what changed everything: his family didn't give up on him. They didn't just pray about him. They prayed for him. They prayed *seeing him whole*. They pictured it. Believed it. Called it into being with the kind of love that reflects the Father Himself. And in time, their faith cracked open the shell of darkness that had held him back for more than a decade.

A Ray of Light in the Hospital Room

Eventually, the pressure became too much, and the founder ended up in a mental hospital. But sometimes, even there—in the quietest, strangest places—God shows up with thunder. One afternoon, in the middle of his stay, something shifted. It wasn't dramatic, but it was undeniable. A small ray of light—literal light—shone into the room. It felt like God Himself was peeking through a tiny spiritual window.

And with that light came a word. A thought. A message so personal, he knew it wasn't from himself: *"Witness to others."* That one idea—that one moment—became the beginning of a new journey. Something clicked. It wasn't a full deliverance. It wasn't a dramatic escape from pain. But it was a spark. A seed. A beginning.

When he was released, the hospital only permitted him to go one place: his parents' house. It wasn't ideal. It didn't feel like success. But it was safe. And sometimes, God brings you low—not to punish you, but to reset your foundation. It was there, in his parents' home, that things started to shift.

Not quickly. Not perfectly. But with momentum.

The Moment Everything Changed: "Put God First Place"

During those first few weeks back home, he started tuning into messages from Joel Osteen. Nothing deep. Nothing theological. But every message ended the same way: *"Find a good Bible-based church and put God first place."* That phrase repeated itself in his heart like a drumbeat.

"Put God first place."

He realized he hadn't been doing that—not for years. In his early twenties, church had stopped feeling useful. He drifted. Slowly at first. Then completely. For almost two decades, his connection to God was background noise. But in his thirties, as life collapsed around him, he hit a point of desperation. He "made a world in his mind," he said—a mental escape to survive the day. But that world didn't save him. It cracked. And when it cracked, the warfare came roaring in.

He describes that season as *"my life blew up."* Mentally, spiritually, emotionally—he felt destroyed. But from that ground zero moment, something new began: a hunger to return to God. And not just casually. Not just church on Sundays. But daily. Deeply. Obsessively. He wanted to keep God in front of his mind at all times.

And so the question became: *How do I do that?*

The Spark That Became the First Deck

In that search, he remembered something. Years earlier, in a totally different context, he had seen a deck of themed playing cards—used for business motivation and productivity. That image stuck with him. What if, he thought, he could make something like that... but for God?

Not a game. A tool. A reminder. Something tactile. Something visual. Something he could actually hold. A way to keep scripture in front of him every day—not as a burden, but as a comfort.

That's when the idea of Scripture Playing Cards came to life.

His first inspiration came from a Bible he had seen in the mental hospital—a small New Testament. On the back of that Bible was a section titled *"The ABC's of Salvation."* He had read through it, fascinated. Each letter of the alphabet corresponded to a verse or phrase related to salvation. He journaled his favorite ones. And now, back home, he pulled out those notes. Could this be the starting point?

He used ChatGPT—an AI tool—to help refine the verses and organize the ideas. He carefully designed layouts using a simple graphic tool. It wasn't fancy. It wasn't even commercial. It was personal. But something about it felt sacred. Scripture. Art. Prayer. Design. Purpose.

And when he printed them—something in him felt healed.

A Simple Deck... That Changed Everything

At first, it was just one deck: *The ABCs of Salvation*. Then came *The ABCs of Prayer*. Then ideas for more. Friends and family started asking questions. Could they try it? Could they get their own? Before he knew it, a personal project was becoming something larger.

Christian Decks was born.

This wasn't about flashy branding or aggressive marketing. It was about solving a real problem: how to keep God first place when your mind is scattered, your past is messy, and your routines are still rebuilding. And this little deck—something you could hold in your hand—was the perfect solution.

It became a daily devotional without pressure. A teaching tool without a lecture. A game that's also a faith-builder. It turned fun into something spiritually meaningful—and made scripture the center of social time, not an awkward interruption.

And that's when he realized: this isn't just helpful. This could be a movement.

The Word of God Is Meant to Be Shared—and Enjoyed

The Bible isn't meant to live only on dusty bookshelves or inside smartphone apps. It's meant to live in our hands. On our lips. Around our dinner tables. That's what these cards make possible. It's truth you can touch. Encouragement you can pass around. Faith you can gift.

The New Testament is filled with evidence—historical records, Roman documentation, eyewitness accounts—all pointing to the life, death, and resurrection of Jesus. And in this modern world, we need to ground ourselves in that same Truth again. These cards help us do that.

They're not replacements for the Bible. They're reminders of it. Carriers of it. Fun, light-hearted, but packed with meaning.

The founder believes in this so deeply that he's already working on more Christian games. Because fun and faith shouldn't be strangers. The early church broke bread together *daily*—not just to preach, but to enjoy. We need more ways to enjoy God's Word together. To build community. To laugh, play, grow, and learn—with Jesus at the center.

Christian Decks makes that possible. And this was just the beginning.

A Movement Was Born—And You're Part of It

It all started with pain. Then a prayer. Then a card. And now—it's a project people all over the world can step into.

Christian Decks isn't just a product. It's a purpose. It's a call to remember the Word. To live by it. To share it. To build something meaningful, profitable, and spiritual—*all at once*.

You don't need a seminary degree. You don't need inventory. You just need willingness. A heart that says, "Yes, Lord." And one simple tool—a Scripture Deck—can open the door to something life-changing.

In the next chapter, we'll explore how these small cards—these *God Reminders*—can bring the Kingdom of Heaven closer to Earth. Because when you hold the Word of God in your hand, and in your conversations, you're not just growing personally. You're planting seeds of revival.

Chapter 3 – "God Reminders": How Scripture Cards Can Bring the Kingdom of Heaven to the Earth

When the Word is visible, the Kingdom becomes real.

The Battle for Your Attention

We live in a world that is fighting for your focus. Ads flash. Notifications ding. Screens glow all day long, shouting for your time. In this environment, even the most committed believer can find it hard to keep their mind fixed on the things of God. That's not because we don't love God—it's because we're surrounded by noise.

The truth is, your spiritual life doesn't grow just because you want it to. It grows when you keep it *in view*. That's why the Bible constantly tells us to "meditate on the Word day and night," to "write it on the doorposts of our homes," and to "bind it to our hands." Why? Because God knows we forget. We drift. We get distracted.

That's what makes Scripture Cards so powerful. They are not just decorations. They are *God Reminders*—small, physical, intentional anchors that pull your attention back to what really matters. They interrupt the noise of the world and re-center you in the truth of God's Kingdom.

A card on your desk. A verse in your hand. A promise by your coffee cup. These small shifts in what you *see* start to reshape how you *think*. And when your thoughts change, your life follows.

What Are "God Reminders"?

A God Reminder is any intentional trigger that helps bring your mind back to Him. It's something small, yet powerful—a word, a verse, a phrase—that speaks into your moment and realigns your spirit with God's truth. And Scripture Cards are full of them.

They're not just paper and ink. They're designed to carry spiritual weight. When you read a verse that says, *"My God shall supply all your needs,"* it's not a suggestion. It's a spiritual reset. A truth injection. It cuts through fear and lack. It reminds you who your Provider is.

When you hold a card that says, *"I can do all things through Christ who strengthens me,"* it shifts your atmosphere. Your mindset. Your posture. You're no longer operating from weakness—you're standing in promise.

And when you give that same card to someone else? You're planting truth in their life. It's more than a gift—it's a seed. A silent sermon. A spark of hope. That's why we call these cards *God Reminders*. Because that's exactly what they are.

Little Cards, Big Kingdom

The Kingdom of Heaven is not just a place—it's a reality. A system. A way of life that reflects God's love, truth, power, and presence. Jesus didn't say, *"Run from this world and hide."* He said, *"Bring the Kingdom here."* "On Earth, as it is in Heaven."

So how do we do that? Through everyday obedience. Through faith in action. Through bringing God's Word into people's everyday moments. That's what Scripture Cards help us do. They bring Heaven closer. Quietly. Lovingly. Powerfully.

Every time someone pulls a card and reads a promise, Heaven gets a little louder in their heart. Every time a family reads a verse together at the dinner table, Heaven moves into that home. Every time a person gives a card to someone hurting, they become a vessel of comfort—and Heaven touches Earth again.

These aren't gimmicks. This is discipleship. This is spiritual formation. This is a new way to spread the Gospel—not by preaching louder, but by inserting God's truth into the center of daily life. It's evangelism through encouragement. Discipleship through design. Fun that fuels faith.

You are literally spreading the Word of God. One verse at a time. One handoff at a time. One smile at a time.

The Power of Visibility

We've been trained to think that spiritual growth happens mostly through quiet time alone or church once a week. But the truth is, we are transformed by what we *see every day*. If you want to grow in faith, change what surrounds you. Change what fills your eyes.

Scripture Cards act like spiritual billboards for your soul. Leave one on your mirror, and your mindset changes before you even leave the house. Place one by your keys, and you walk out the door remembering who you are in Christ. Tuck one into your Bible, and every time you read, you're greeted with fresh encouragement.

This is how you *abide* in the Word. Not once a week. Not once a month. But daily. Naturally. With joy. The more you see truth, the more it becomes part of you. And when that happens, you start living differently—speaking differently—believing differently.

You don't need more effort. You need more reminders.

You don't need guilt. You need focus.

And God has already given us the tool: His Word.

The Future of Christian Decks

What if you had a different deck for every need? What if you could build a Scripture Deck specifically designed for healing? Or hope? Or wealth-building? Or business success? What if you could carry a set of verses tailored to your next season—and hand out encouragement as easily as playing a card?

That's the future of Christian Decks. We're not stopping with one idea. This is the beginning of a catalog of *God Reminders*—custom decks designed to speak into the exact needs people are facing. Decks for youth ministries. Decks for marriage groups. Decks for healing rooms. Decks for missionaries. Decks for new believers.

Each deck becomes a devotional in disguise. A toolkit. A game that teaches truth. A faith-builder that doesn't feel forced. A family activity that leads to transformation.

We're also building out interactive ways to use them: scavenger hunts with scripture cards. Memory games for kids. "Draw-a-verse" discipleship nights. There is no limit to what can happen when God's Word becomes central in how we play, relate, and communicate.

This is just the beginning.

Turning Your Cards into Mini-Devotionals

Imagine waking up and drawing a card from your deck. It says, *"Delight yourself in the Lord, and He will give you the desires of your heart."* You read it. Then on the back, there's a simple question: *"What's one desire you need to lay before Him today?"*

That's a devotional. And you didn't open a book or sit through a lesson. You just engaged with the Word in real-time. That's the power of supercharged Scripture Cards. With just a few added prompts or applications, these decks can become full-on mini-devotionals—custom built for your life and your calling.

Use them in your quiet time. Share them with your church group. Turn them into a journaling prompt. Or bring them to a coffee shop and let God lead the conversation. These aren't static cards—they're living tools.

We're designing more of these formats right now. And as the Christian Decks community grows, more variations will appear—because God is creative, and His Word is infinite. Each deck is a new way to engage with the same eternal truth.

God's Word Is the Most Powerful Thing on Earth

This is more than a business. It's more than a product. It's a delivery system for God's Word. And there's nothing more powerful, nothing more healing, and nothing more effective than the spoken Word of God.

Scripture tells us that "the Word of God is living and active, sharper than any two-edged sword." When you carry a Scripture Deck, you're not just carrying cards—you're carrying weapons. Seeds. Promises. Fire.

And when you give one to someone else? You're giving them something that never expires. Something that will speak again and again. Something the Holy Spirit can use at any time.

So start using your deck daily. Start carrying it with you. Keep it in your car. Keep it in your bag. Use it for you—and then offer it to others.

Because when God's Word shows up everywhere, the Kingdom starts showing up everywhere too.

Chapter 4 – "The Call of God": Why This Is More Than a Business – It's a Mission

You're not just launching a business. You're answering Heaven's call.

What if Your Business Was Also Your Ministry?

For many Christians, the word "business" feels separate from the word "ministry." Business is how we make money. Ministry is how we serve. But what if that separation was never meant to exist? What if, instead, your business *could become* your ministry—because the core of it was spreading the Word of God?

That's exactly what Christian Decks offers. Yes, it's a product. Yes, there's income potential. But underneath it all, it's something much deeper: a tool for discipleship. A vessel for evangelism. A delivery system for Truth. You're not just selling cards—you're sowing scripture into people's daily lives.

This is what makes it a mission. It's not just about transactions. It's about transformation. Each time someone pulls a card and reads a verse, they're connecting with God. They're hearing His promises. They're stepping into Kingdom perspective. And you played a role in that.

That's the mission: to get more of God's Word into more hands, hearts, and homes. To normalize the presence of scripture in everyday life. And to give Christians a tool that's easy to use, powerful to share, and joyful to carry.

A New Way to Fulfill the Great Commission

Jesus didn't suggest we go make disciples—He commanded it. In Matthew 28:19–20, He said:

"Go therefore and make disciples of all nations, baptizing them... teaching them to observe all that I have commanded you."

This isn't optional. It's the central assignment for every believer. But for most people, the question isn't *"Should I do it?"*—it's *"How can I do it?"* Not everyone is called to preach. Not everyone is trained to teach. But everyone can share. Everyone can plant a seed.

Scripture Cards give you that opportunity. You don't have to lead a sermon—you just need to hand someone a verse. That's teaching. That's disciple-making. That's obedience to Jesus' call.

And when you build a Mutual Success Team around that effort, you multiply that impact. Every person on your team becomes part of the mission. Every card distributed is another moment where someone meets the Word of God.

You're not just starting a company. You're starting a ripple of Kingdom obedience that can reach farther than you think.

---

5 Scriptures That Define the Mission

This chapter wouldn't be complete without grounding this mission in the Word. Below are five foundational scriptures that define what we're doing, why it matters, and how it connects directly to God's calling for His people:

1. **Matthew 28:19-20 (The Great Commission)**

"Go therefore and make disciples of all nations... teaching them..."
This is our instruction from Jesus Himself—to teach others. And these cards are a portable teaching tool, usable by anyone, anywhere.

2. **John 13:34-35 (Love One Another)**

"By this everyone will know that you are my disciples, if you love one another."
True love means caring for others' spiritual needs. Handing someone the truth in a moment of weakness *is* love in action.

3. **Acts 2:44-45 (Kingdom Sharing)**

"All the believers were together and had everything in common... they sold property and possessions to give to anyone who had need."
The early church was radically generous—and united. Our Mutual Success Teams echo this call: to work together so there is "no need among them."

4. **Romans 10:17 (Faith Comes by Hearing)**

"Faith comes by hearing, and hearing by the Word of Christ."
Every card read is a chance for faith to rise. These decks multiply faith—quietly, daily, powerfully.

5. **Hebrews 10:24-25 (Spurring One Another On)**

"Let us consider how we may spur one another on toward love and good deeds... encouraging one another."
These cards are a tool of encouragement. They stir up the body of Christ to keep growing, believing, and doing.

Each of these verses points to one clear truth: We are called to *do* something with our faith. Christian Decks give us the "how."

This Is About Family—Your Christian Family

When Jesus was teaching one day, someone told Him, "Your mother and brothers are outside." His response was shocking. He said:

"Who is my mother, and who are my brothers?"
"Here are my mother and my brothers! For whoever does the will of my Father in heaven is my brother and sister and mother." (Matthew 12:48–50)

Jesus redefined family. He showed us that our spiritual family—those who follow Him—are just as important, if not more, than our earthly relatives. That means when we support the body of Christ, we're caring for *our* family. When we bring scripture into someone's life, we're feeding our brothers and sisters.

And here's the radical truth: if you help build someone's faith, you are fulfilling your role as spiritual family. If you help someone grow in God, stay encouraged, or build a God-centered business, you're caring for your household—the family of believers.

Christian Decks empower you to do that easily, naturally, and powerfully.

A Business That Fulfills a Higher Purpose

Let's get honest for a moment. Most businesses are built around "more." More money. More clients. More visibility. But this mission is about *better.* Better conversations. Better communities. Better access to truth. Better tools for believers to grow and give.

Of course, there's income potential here. God is not against profit—He's against selfishness. What we're building is not selfish. It's rooted in love, service, and Kingdom strategy. You earn not to hoard, but to bless. You prosper not to show off, but to support the work of God and meet needs in His family.

That's why Mutual Success Teams matter. Because you're not trying to become rich *alone.* You're rising *with others.* You're teaching, equipping, and modeling a way of success that actually reflects God's values.

And when more of God's people live that way? We begin to fulfill the vision of Acts 4:34:

"There was not a needy person among them."

That's the endgame.

The Mission Is Ours—And It Starts Now

This chapter is your reminder: this isn't just a product. It's a mission. This isn't just something you do for side income. It's something you do for *eternal* impact.

Christian Decks give us a modern tool to fulfill an ancient calling: bring God's Word into the lives of others—consistently, lovingly, practically.

You don't need to be a pastor. You don't need to preach. You just need to care. To act. To hand someone a verse that speaks life. That shifts a day. That builds belief.

We are the body of Christ. And the mission is still the same:

- Make disciples
- Teach truth
- Love deeply
- Meet needs
- Build community
- And spread the Kingdom

You now have a tool to do that. So pick it up. Carry it. Share it. And let your business become your mission.

Chapter 5 – The Origin of "Team Success" & the "Mutual Success Team"

The idea that flipped everything—and made financial overflow finally possible

---

Where the Breakthrough Really Began

It started with a simple, unsettling realization: Most people are trained not to succeed—*together*. From our earliest years, we were taught that asking for help is cheating. That sharing ideas is suspicious. That teaming up for success is somehow unfair. But what if the very rules we were given were based on the wrong world?

In school, we were warned: Don't copy. Don't share answers. Don't help your neighbor. And those warnings were meant to protect academic integrity, of course—but they carried a subtle poison: the belief that independence is the only honest path to achievement.

Then you step into real life, and suddenly the opposite is true. Business leaders rise because of their teams. Entrepreneurs partner to scale. Churches thrive through shared effort. Collaborating is no longer dangerous—it's essential.

That's where the idea of *Team Success* came from. Not rebellion. Not ego. But reflection. And it led to one powerful, defining question:

What if we stopped calling it cheating—and started calling it what it really is?

Mutual success.

The Day We Flipped the Script

The founder of Christian Decks wrestled with this question deeply. Like many of us, he had spent most of his life believing success had to be earned solo. Asking for help felt weak. Sharing breakthroughs felt risky. Collaboration felt like a compromise.

But then he asked a better question: *What if collaboration wasn't a weakness? What if it was the Kingdom model all along?*

The answer came back strong, through prayer, through scripture, and even through wise insight from AI-powered tools. A new idea was born—Team Success. A concept that takes what the world calls "cheating" and redefines it through the lens of love, service, and strategy. A framework where we build something great *together*, not just for one, but for all.

That's how the first Mutual Success Team began—not as a company, not as a project, but as a *model*. A new ethic. A new way to win that doesn't leave others behind. A way of working that reflects the Gospel's own generosity.

It started with one person deciding: I will no longer compete alone. I will rise with others. And that decision changed everything.

What Exactly Is a Mutual Success Team?

Let's define it clearly. A **Mutual Success Team** is a group of people who agree to grow together—with open hands, open hearts, and open strategy. It's not a club. It's not a committee. It's a collaboration covenant. The simple belief that if we help each other succeed, we'll all get there faster—and stronger.

Each Mutual Success Team is committed to:

- Sharing knowledge and breakthroughs
- Brainstorming solutions and ideas together
- Offering practical help, feedback, and support
- Measuring success not just by personal gain—but by collective growth
- Staying aligned with biblical values of honesty, service, and generosity

There's no jealousy here. No hoarding. No scarcity thinking. Just a shared belief that we all rise when we rise together. That's the essence of *Team Success.*

And here's the real power behind it: **It works.**
This isn't just a theory. The founder of Christian Decks saw personal financial increase, sustained momentum, and even deeper spiritual strength the moment he embraced this idea—and lived it out.

Why Team Success Is So Revolutionary (And So Needed)

Let's be honest: Most of us were programmed by the world's scarcity system. The idea that *"If you win, I lose."* That's a lie. God's Kingdom operates in abundance. The Bible teaches that *"there was no need among them"* in the early church—not because everyone was rich individually, but because everyone shared what they had.

That's the model.

We're not meant to hoard blessings. We're meant to circulate them. When someone on your team has a breakthrough, that's not a threat—it's a gift to the whole group. When someone makes $1,000 this month selling Scripture Decks, that's not competition—it's proof that you can too.

Team Success teaches us to celebrate together, learn together, and rise together. It reprograms us from solo success to shared overflow. From comparison to collaboration. From isolation to multiplication.

And here's what it leads to: **permanent cash flow**. Not the kind that fades with one campaign or a single sale. But the kind that flows through systems, through relationships, and through consistent mutual effort. That's what Mutual Success Teams are built to generate.

Financial Overflow Is Not Just Possible—It's Designed

The world says passive income is for the lucky few. But in the Kingdom, income should be rooted in purpose, community, and divine strategy. Mutual Success Teams unlock this because they allow each member to share what's working—and everyone benefits.

Let's say one person discovers how to sell Christian Decks through a local homeschool group. They share the process. Others replicate it. Now instead of one person earning $500, the team is earning $5,000 together. That's Team Success.

This mindset flips everything:

- From secret-keeping to strategy-sharing
- From solo sales to team-based promotions
- From temporary wins to lasting momentum

That's how overflow begins—not through constant hustle, but through trusted teamwork. When each person gives what they've learned, the whole team becomes stronger. And the success begins to flow in ways that surprise you.

You stop scrambling. You stop burning out. You start *receiving*—because you're giving, and because you're surrounded by others doing the same.

The Spiritual Root of Mutual Success

This isn't just a smart business idea. It's a biblical one.

God never designed us to succeed alone. Even Jesus didn't work alone—He had 12 disciples, and He sent them out *two by two*. Paul traveled with teams. The early church met daily, shared everything, and ensured *"there was no need among them."* (Acts 4:34)

Here's what the Bible tells us about true success:

- *"Two are better than one... a cord of three strands is not quickly broken."* (Ecclesiastes 4:9–12)
- *"Carry each other's burdens, and in this way you will fulfill the law of Christ."* (Galatians 6:2)
- *"Now the body is not made up of one part but of many."* (1 Corinthians 12:14)

The truth is, every great move of God in history came from groups. From agreement. From shared focus. From teams. Team Success is not a new gimmick—it's a return to that original Kingdom design.

And now, through something as simple as Scripture Cards, you get to activate that model again—right in your city, your church, your community.

Team Success Is the Movement—And You're In It

This chapter is more than a history lesson. It's a call. A chance to leave behind the isolation of "doing everything on your own," and step into something better.

A *Mutual Success Team* can become your new launchpad.
A place to test, grow, and multiply what's working—while being supported by others on the same journey.

It's not just a great idea. It's a proven path.

You don't have to carry the vision alone.
You don't have to build the business alone.
You don't have to celebrate the wins alone.

There's a team waiting to grow with you. And as you grow together, you'll see overflow—spiritually, relationally, and financially.

Let's keep going. The next chapter will show you how your first Mutual Success Project—selling Christian Decks—can set all of this in motion.

Chapter 6 – "Mutual Success Team": Your First Project – Earn While Spreading the Word in a Way That Fits You Perfectly

A business made for believers, built for overflow, and designed to fit your God-given life

---

This Is Your First Mutual Success Project

If you've ever dreamed of starting something meaningful… if you've ever wanted to earn income while doing Kingdom work… if you've ever wished there was a business that didn't feel forced, didn't require high pressure sales, and didn't compromise your values—this is it.

This is your first *Mutual Success Project.*

It's simple. It's powerful. And it's ready to begin today. At the center of it all is one product: a Scripture Deck. A small, hold-it-in-your-hand tool that spreads the Word of God and starts conversations that matter.

But this isn't just about the deck—it's about the model behind it. You're not just selling a product. You're launching a *Mutual Success Team*. That means you're doing it with others, learning as you go, helping people, and building a business that reflects God's way of creating impact: **together**.

This is the project that proves you don't have to compromise in order to succeed. You just have to start.

There Are 100+ Ways to Win—Just Pick One

You don't have to invent your own method. You don't have to guess what might work. Because we're giving you over **100+ different ways** to share and sell Christian Decks. Yes, 100+.

In Part 4 of this book, you'll find the full list—categorized, explained, and matched to different types of people and lifestyles. Whether you're introverted or outgoing, creative or analytical, tech-savvy or totally offline—there's a way that fits you.

This is what makes this different from any other business. You're not forced into one rigid system. You're handed a toolkit and shown how to make it your own. No cold calling. No manipulation. Just real methods for real people—doing what they already love to do.

And that's what makes this *easy*.

Not in the sense of "no work"—but in the sense of *aligned work*. Work that doesn't burn you out. Work that doesn't make you feel like someone you're not. You get to earn while being fully you. Fully authentic. Fully aligned with your mission and message.

That's not common. But it's Kingdom.

From Side Project to Overflow: The $10K Potential

Let's talk numbers. Because this isn't just a mission—it's a financial opportunity. One that's proven to work. One that can create **permanent cash flow**—not just for you, but for your whole team.

Most people aim for side income. A few hundred extra a month. That's great. But a *Mutual Success Project* is built to go farther. When you work together with others, share your best strategies, and build consistent rhythms—you can reach $10,000 per month or more.

That's not hype. That's math.

Let's say you sell decks that earn you $10 to $15 profit each. Selling 5 a day gets you to $1,500–$2,250 a month. Multiply that with team members. Multiply that with methods that scale—like digital sales, events, or affiliate systems—and suddenly you're looking at overflow.

Not just income. **Predictable cash flow**. Money you can rely on. Money that comes from doing something *good*. Something *holy*. Something that makes the world better and brings the Word of God into more lives.

That's what makes this special. It's not about being rich. It's about being free. Financially free. Spiritually full. Impacting others—and doing it with a team that's cheering you on.

You Don't Have to Do This Alone

What makes most businesses fail isn't the product. It's the pressure. It's the isolation. The feeling of having to figure it all out by yourself. That's not how we do things here.

When you start this project, you're invited to build a *Mutual Success Team*. That means your own circle of people who want to grow, give, and earn together. You're not just selling a card—you're modeling a lifestyle. You're showing others what it looks like to build something that matters.

Your Mutual Success Team could be made up of:

- Friends from church
- Family members who want to earn with purpose
- Young people looking for mentorship
- Moms, students, retirees—anyone with a heart to serve

You don't need to be a business expert to lead. You just need willingness. We give you the training, the scripts, the meeting templates. Everything you need to start. And as you grow, so does your team. As you succeed, you invite others into that same success.

That's why we call it *mutual*. Everyone wins—because everyone helps.

This Project Was Made for People Like You

You may be wondering: *Can I really do this?*

Let's answer that honestly. Yes.

Because this project was made for people who care. Who love God. Who want to make a difference. Who maybe never saw themselves as entrepreneurs, but who know deep down that they're called to more.

You don't need a degree. You don't need money upfront. You just need desire—and a willingness to take one step at a time.

This isn't a high-pressure sales gig. It's a low-friction mission. The product is scripture. The purpose is Kingdom. The reward is both financial and eternal.

And you're not being thrown into this alone. You're being equipped—with clarity, community, and tools. When was the last time a company handed you 100+ ways to win, and said, "Pick the one that feels like you"?

That's what you have now. Use it.

What Happens When You Say Yes

When you say yes to this Mutual Success Project, here's what starts to happen:

- You begin sharing scripture—without pressure, in ways that feel natural.
- You earn income—in proportion to your action, not your anxiety.
- You gain confidence—because you're finally doing something aligned.
- You attract others—who want to join in, because they see your peace and purpose.
- You build momentum—because you're no longer trying to do everything alone.

And over time, something bigger happens: you change your financial future. You build something you can hand down. You create a model others can copy. You become a leader of overflow.

All from one small deck. All from one small step.

Ready for the Next Step?

This chapter is your invitation. It's your open door. The path is in front of you—and the methods are laid out in Part 4.

So here's what you do:

1. **Decide to start**. You don't need to know everything. Just start.
2. **Pick one method** (out of 100+) that feels easy for you.
3. **Share your story** with a friend or two. Invite them to join your team.
4. **Track your results**, and let momentum grow from there.

This is your first Mutual Success Project. But it won't be your last.

You're not just earning. You're equipping. You're building something that can't be shaken.

Welcome to the movement. Welcome to Team Success.

Chapter 7 – What Makes This & You Different? "Mutual Success" Is a New Powerful Idea

You weren't built for isolation. You were built for multiplied success.

This Is a New Kind of Success Story

What if your success wasn't about you rising alone—but about others rising *with you*?

That's the difference with this. It's not a hustle. It's not a solo grind. It's not another dream of "making it big" while everyone else watches. This is about building something together—on purpose, for purpose. This is what makes you and this project *different*.

You're not stepping into just another business model. You're stepping into a **Mutual Success Mindset**. That mindset changes everything. It transforms the way you work, the way you think, the way you measure progress, and the way you help others.

You're not here to fight your way to the top. You're here to build something wide, lasting, and relational—with others who want to do the same.

And the truth is: this is the *strongest foundation* for real business success that never burns out.

The Old Model: Individualism and Scarcity

Let's name the problem most of us grew up with: *individualism.*

Do it on your own. Figure it out by yourself. Keep your secrets. Don't rely on anyone. That mindset sounds strong... until you hit your first wall. Until you realize that every major breakthrough in the real world happens through *collaboration*.

And underneath that individualism? A scarcity mindset. The belief that if someone else wins, it somehow takes something away from you. The fear that there's only so much success to go around. That it's a zero-sum game.

But here's the good news: **that's a lie.**

In God's Kingdom, success is not limited. In fact, success is *multiplied* when it's shared. That's what Mutual Success is all about.

You get to leave those broken ideas behind. No more proving yourself. No more protecting your knowledge. No more scarcity panic.

From now on, you do things *with people*. You build *together*. You rise *together*. You earn *together*. And when you win, you make sure others win too.

That's how this model works. And that's why it doesn't break.

The Two Decisions That Will Change Your Life

Let's keep it simple. The entire idea of Mutual Success boils down to **two life-changing decisions**:

1. **Decide to collaborate for the mutual success of everyone involved.**
2. **Decide to never build something alone again.**

That's it.

Those two choices are enough to transform your future. They are the *antidote* to years of disappointment. They undo the lonely failure of past attempts. They break the cycle of solo effort and burnout.

Why?

Because when you share your knowledge, others grow. When others grow, they share back. When they succeed, you're encouraged. When you succeed, they're inspired. It creates a feedback loop of *perpetual growth*. And that's what makes this model so stable.

Mutual Success is not about charity. It's about *compound success*. The more you give, the more you receive. The more you include, the more momentum you create.

That's how you build a $10k/month business that lasts. That's how you create a network that others *want* to join. That's how you change lives—starting with your own.

Five Strengths That Make This Business Model Work

Let's dig into the strengths behind this system. These aren't just features. These are *pillars*—the five things that make Mutual Success Teams unstoppable when practiced together:

1. Built-In Collaboration
No one has to figure it out alone. Everyone contributes what they've learned. You're not just duplicating a product—you're duplicating *insight*. That makes it easier, faster, and more joyful.

2. Deep Personalization
You don't need to copy someone else's method. You get to choose from over 100+ proven strategies and make it fit *you*. This flexibility removes the pressure and unlocks creativity.

3. Consistent Encouragement
Mutual Success Teams don't just trade tips—they encourage each other. They pray together. They laugh, brainstorm, and celebrate together. That emotional fuel is a game-changer.

4. Shared Wins, Shared Momentum
When one person succeeds, they bring the whole team with them. A breakthrough in one corner of the group becomes a door for everyone. This creates *scalable momentum* that doesn't depend on one superstar.

5. Kingdom-Centered Values
This isn't a cutthroat business model. It's rooted in biblical principles—generosity, stewardship, service, and faith. That makes it trustworthy, sustainable, and anointed.

These five things combined create an ecosystem where people don't just survive in business—they *thrive.*

Stay in the Mutual Success Mindset

This isn't just something you *do*—it's a way of thinking you *keep.* The Mutual Success Mindset is a daily decision to remember why you started and who you're building with.

Here's how to stay in that mindset:

- **Think "we," not "me."** Before every decision, ask: *How does this help my team, too?*

- **Share what's working.** Don't hoard insights. Teach others. Let your win be their next step.
- **Celebrate others as much as yourself.** Their success doesn't steal from you—it *builds you.*
- **Create tools that serve others.** Ask, *Does what I'm building empower someone else?*
- **Stay centered on the Word.** The Kingdom isn't built on personality—it's built on truth.

And remember this: every time you help someone else succeed, you are strengthening the foundation of your own business. That's the miracle of Mutual Success.

How This Project Helps Everyone Involved

The more you think about it, the more this entire business becomes a Team Success Tool.

Selling Scripture Decks? That spreads the Word.

Building a team? That spreads financial stability.

Teaching what worked for you? That spreads insight.

Helping others launch? That spreads belief.

You're not just handing out cards—you're handing out hope, faith, encouragement, and opportunity. Every person who touches this business is better because of it. That's the Mutual Success effect.

This is why the product is only the beginning. The real product is *the change in people*. You get to create a ripple effect of transformation—because you chose not to do it alone.

That's what makes this so different. And that's what makes *you* different, too.

You're Not Like the Rest—And That's the Point

Other business models try to force you into a mold. They want you to hustle harder, sell more aggressively, and win by outcompeting everyone around you.

But you're not here to hustle. You're here to help.

You're not here to compete. You're here to *collaborate.*

You're not here to win alone. You're here to *win with others.*

That's your advantage. That's your strength. And that's what will make this business feel *right* in your spirit—because it's aligned with the way God intended us to grow.

You're different. This is different. And that's the best news you've heard in a long time.

Ready to Take This to the Next Level?

Now that you understand the mindset, it's time to lead with it. Your product is more than a deck. It's a door. A door into Kingdom collaboration, overflow, and transformation.

So ask yourself:

- How will I share this mindset today?
- Who can I build with?
- Where can I create a small win—for me and someone else?

That's Mutual Success in motion.

You're not just doing business. You're doing something sacred. Something shared. Something better.

Welcome to the new way.

Chapter 8 – Being Willing to Mentor Others & Share Everything

If it worked for you, it can work for someone else—and the Kingdom is counting on it.

What If Your Breakthrough Could Be Someone Else's Beginning?

One of the most powerful things you can do in this journey is also one of the simplest: *share what worked for you*. That alone can change someone's life. It can unlock new income, spark new vision, and even heal old doubts. Because when someone sees that it worked for you—*just as you are*—they begin to believe it could work for them too.

This chapter isn't about being a guru. It's not about being an expert or having all the answers. It's about being available. Being honest. Being *willing*. Willing to mentor others. Willing to share your process. Willing to say, "Here's exactly how I did it—maybe this can help you too."

That's the heart of Team Success. It's not built on superstars. It's built on servants. People who show up, share truth, and walk alongside others until they win.

So if you've found a method that works for selling Christian Decks—write it down. If you've built momentum with your Mutual Success Team—document the steps. That knowledge isn't just yours. It belongs to the Body. And when you give it away, you multiply it.

Mentorship Doesn't Mean Perfection—It Means Clarity

Too many people hesitate to mentor others because they think, *"I haven't figured it all out yet."* But that's not what mentoring is about. It's not about being perfect. It's about being *clear*. Clear about what you've tried. Clear about what worked. Clear about what didn't.

Mentorship doesn't require you to be the expert. It requires you to be *real*. And when you lead from authenticity, people lean in. They listen. They try. Because you didn't hand them a fantasy. You handed them something they could actually use.

So here's your job: write down what's working. Make a simple list. Step-by-step. No fluff. No exaggeration. Just a duplicatable version of your experience. Then do two things with it:

(A) Share it with *one person*. A friend. A teammate. Someone curious but unsure. Walk them through it.

(B) Send it to the *Team Success Network*. We'll soon be providing a formal template you can use to make this process easy, so your success can become part of the global toolkit we're building.

Because what worked for you, someone else is praying for right now.

You're Helping Build the System That Will End Global Need

Let's step back for a second. What are we *really* doing here?

We're not just starting businesses. We're building a system. A model. A replicable, faithful, Holy-Spirit-led way of creating income through Kingdom mission. And we want that model to be so duplicatable, so simple, so powerful—that it could be picked up by anyone, anywhere, and used to create lasting provision.

Why? Because of Acts 4:34:

"There were no needy persons among them."

That's what the early church looked like. And that's what we're aiming for again. Not in theory. In real life.

We envision a world where churches are not struggling to fund their ministries. Where families are not crushed by financial stress. Where Christians are free to build, give, and serve without constantly worrying about their bills. And how do we get there?

We get there through *models that can be shared*. Through Mutual Success Projects that are real, profitable, and teachable. Through mentors like you who say, "Here's exactly how I did it. Try this next."

This is how the Kingdom comes—through obedience, simplicity, and replication.

Your Efforts Are Answering God's Call to Care for His People

The Bible is clear: we are responsible for each other. We're not just called to preach. We're called to *provide*. Not just to comfort people in need—but to *eliminate the need altogether.*

In 1 John 3:17, the Word says:

"If anyone has material possessions and sees a brother or sister in need but has no pity on them, how can the love of God be in that person?"

Ouch. That verse is direct. And it's not there to guilt us. It's there to remind us of who we really are: **a family.**

And if we're a family, then what you build *matters*. Not just for you, but for the people you'll eventually help. That's why documenting what worked for you—and mentoring someone else with it—isn't a bonus task. It's central to the mission.

You're not just making money. You're preparing a model that can provide *generational impact*. A system that can lift others out of survival and into Kingdom purpose. A tool that could be handed off to a local church, a youth ministry, or a family in crisis—anywhere in the world.

Your part in that matters more than you realize.

This Is How the Kingdom Multiplies

Jesus didn't just heal and preach. He *taught*. He passed on everything to the disciples, who then taught others, who taught others still. That's why we're here today—because someone shared what worked.

That's the pattern. That's the multiplication model. And it starts with simple acts of mentorship.

You don't need a classroom. Just a phone call.

You don't need a curriculum. Just your story.

You don't need credentials. Just your heart.

And the moment you step into that role, you're not just a business builder—you're a discipler. A leader. A Kingdom connector. You're equipping the saints for the work of ministry, even if you've never thought of yourself that way.

That's what Mutual Success unlocks. Not just earnings, but *legacy*. Not just change for you, but change for someone else—*through you*.

You Don't Need to Wait—You Can Start Mentoring Now

You might be thinking, *"Okay... but when do I do this?"*

The answer is: *now*. You already know enough. You've already learned something valuable. So here's how to get started this week:

1. **Write down your method.** Make it clear. What did you do? In what order? How did it help?
2. **Choose one person.** Someone interested, watching, or quietly struggling.
3. **Offer to walk them through it.** No pressure. No pitch. Just help.
4. **Let the Team Success Network know.** Soon, we'll be publishing shared stories and systems from the field. Yours could help thousands.

You don't have to change the world in one day. Just teach what you've already lived. That's more than enough.

The Ripple Effect of Shared Success

When one person learns a method that works and shares it with another, who then shares it with five more... a movement begins. A quiet, holy revolution of generosity and wisdom.

And that's what we're building. A new era of church-supported entrepreneurship. A network of believers who grow, give, and mentor—until there is *no need among them*.

You're part of that.

Your wisdom matters.

Your story matters.

Your success matters.

And your willingness to *share everything that worked for you*—might just become the foundation of someone else's future.

Chapter 9 – Why You Should Succeed – Part 1: 7 Reasons Why – What's Stacked in Your Favor

This is a setup for success—and you're standing right in the middle of it.

You're More Ready Than You Think

A lot of people hesitate before starting something new. They wonder, *"Can I really do this?" "What if I fail?" "What if I'm not the business type?"*

But here's what this chapter is about: showing you just how much is already stacked in your favor. You're not walking into this with empty hands. You're stepping into a system that's been designed to make success possible—even likely—for people just like you.

There are seven distinct reasons this works. Not by accident. Not by hype. But because this project was built with you in mind. These aren't abstract concepts. These are practical realities that lower the barrier to entry, remove the fear, and help you step confidently into action.

So if you've ever questioned whether this path is for you, lean in.

Let's walk through the seven reasons why this may be *the most accessible, aligned, and anointed business project you'll ever touch.*

---

1. Simple Product – Everyone Understands Playing Cards

You're not trying to explain a complicated tech service. You're not pitching a strange supplement or abstract opportunity. You're showing someone a deck of cards—and they already know exactly what that is.

The product is instantly familiar. People don't need convincing to hold it, flip through it, or try it out. And that's a huge advantage in business. Because most businesses fail at the very first step: *getting people to understand what you're offering.*

With Scripture Decks, there's no confusion. No mental hurdle. No long sales pitch. Just a familiar format—used in a fresh, life-giving way.

That simplicity builds trust fast. It creates openness. And it makes your work much easier from the start.

---

2. Universal Need – Everyone Needs Encouragement

We live in a world that runs low on hope. People are discouraged, distracted, overwhelmed. Whether they're believers or not, everyone needs encouragement. Everyone needs truth.

And Scripture Decks provide that—in a warm, practical, non-pushy way.

Each card becomes a conversation starter. A lift in someone's day. A spark of faith in a quiet moment. That means your product doesn't just sit on a shelf—it *moves* in people's lives. It's useful. It's wanted. It fills an emotional and spiritual need that most people don't even realize they've been missing.

That's why this product sells so naturally. Because it's not just about faith—it's about *feeling better.* And almost everyone wants that.

---

3. Natural Market – Christians Buy from Christians

Let's talk demographics.

Christians love to support other Christians. It's natural. It's relational. It's value-driven. When believers see a product that lines up with their faith—and supports someone in the Body—they're far more likely to say "yes."

That gives you an enormous edge.

You're not marketing to strangers. You're offering something meaningful to people who already agree with the mission. Churches. Bible studies. Christian families. Ministries. Youth leaders. Homeschoolers. Pastors. Small groups. These are people who actively want to use scripture-centered tools in their homes and communities.

That means the market isn't just big—it's *ready.*

And the best part? It keeps growing. Every person who loves your deck will show it to someone else. Every church that adopts it will become a new hub of customers and partners.

You're not chasing interest. You're stepping into it.

---

4. Relationship-Based – Builds on Existing Connections

This project doesn't require you to cold-call strangers or knock on doors. It works beautifully through your existing relationships.

Think about your circle: friends, family, church members, online groups, local ministries. That's where this starts. You're not just selling a product—you're inviting people into something you're excited about. Something that's helped you. Something that honors God.

And that relational approach builds something stronger than a sale. It builds *trust.*

Plus, it makes every conversation more relaxed. You don't have to be "salesy." You can just be *you*—sharing what you've found, and inviting others into it.

That's not just smart business. That's how the Gospel spreads: *life to life, heart to heart.*

---

5. Scripture-Centered – Appeals to the Christian Community

The Christian world is hungry for tools that are both fun and faith-filled.

Most products are one or the other: they're either spiritually deep but hard to share, or they're entertaining but spiritually shallow. Scripture Decks are different. They bring the Word into daily life—in a format people enjoy.

That makes them *highly appealing* to the Christian community. Parents love them for their kids. Churches love them for small groups. Ministries love them for outreach. Individuals love them for daily encouragement.

And because they're centered on scripture, they carry the highest possible credibility. You're not offering your own opinions—you're offering God's promises.

That makes every deck you share a seed of truth. And the Christian community recognizes that. They see the value. They feel the impact. And they want more.

6. Making Money – People Work for Meaningful Income

Let's be honest: if this didn't make money, most people wouldn't do it. And that's okay. Because in God's Kingdom, provision *matters.* Your time is valuable. Your energy deserves reward. And this project provides a very real income opportunity.

You're not just doing something good—you're getting paid to do it.

Each deck you share becomes a stream of income. And as your team grows, so does your earning potential. When you help others succeed, you succeed. When you scale, you stabilize. And that's how you move from a few dollars a week to a few thousand a month—or more.

This isn't about hype. It's about *structure*. The kind of structure that leads to *lasting* income—based on real value, not tricks.

People will buy what you're offering. And you'll get paid to keep offering it.

7. Team Support – Success Is Shared Responsibility

This isn't a solo mission.

One of the biggest reasons you'll succeed is because you're not doing this alone. You're part of a **Mutual Success Team**. That means when you get stuck, someone helps. When you succeed, someone celebrates. When you figure something out, someone else benefits.

Success becomes shared responsibility.

And that makes everything easier. Less stress. Less guessing. More feedback. More support. More wins—together.

Your team will cheer you on. Share ideas. Offer prayers. Cover you in your weak moments. Multiply your strong ones. And as you do the same for them, your community becomes your engine.

That's why this model *works*. Because the weight isn't all on your shoulders. It's distributed—and lifted—by those who walk with you.

You're Set Up to Win—Now Just Start Walking

These seven reasons are not just bullet points. They are *confirmation*. You've been given a head start. A simplified path. A proven product. A built-in market. A relational launchpad. A spiritual backbone. And a team.

You have everything you need to move forward with confidence.

So stop waiting for the perfect moment. This *is* the moment. Everything is stacked in your favor.

You were born for this kind of success. And the next chapter will show you how it goes even deeper—with the biblical model behind all of it.

Chapter 10 – Why You Should Succeed – Part 2: "The Mutual Success Solution" – What's Stacked In Your Favor?

There's a reason this works—and it goes all the way back to the early church.

You're Not Just Doing Business—You're Following a Proven Model

You don't have to wonder if this approach will work.

It already has.

The original believers—the early church—operated with a model so effective, so radical, and so anointed that it turned the Roman Empire upside down. It wasn't based on marketing. It wasn't built on hierarchy. It didn't require mass advertising or capital investment. It was powered by one core principle: *mutual success.*

And the results? The Bible says in Acts 4:34:

"There was not a needy person among them."

That wasn't a fantasy. That was *real*. It happened. And it happened because the people of God decided to live differently—to share what they had, to look after each other, and to become a network of love, generosity, and shared growth.

Every church was a *Mutual Success Team* before the phrase even existed.

So what does that mean for you?

It means you're not building something new from scratch. You're returning to something that *already worked.* Something biblical. Something time-tested. You're planting your business in soil that's been producing fruit since the Book of Acts.

And now, you get to use that same soil to grow your own Kingdom enterprise.

---

1. The Biblical Model – "There Was No Need Among Them"

Imagine this: a group of believers, full of faith and unity, pooling their time, their gifts, and even their resources—not for control, but for the good of all.

That was the early church.

"All the believers were together and had everything in common... they gave to anyone who had need." (Acts 2:44–45)

They didn't wait for Rome to change. They didn't wait for laws to shift or economies to improve. They *became the solution*—together.

That's what makes the biblical model so powerful: it wasn't dependent on external systems. It was fueled by *internal commitment*—to each other, and to God's Word.

That's what Mutual Success looks like. And that's what you're stepping into. A model where you use what you have—not just for your gain, but for *the gain of all.* And in that environment, *everyone* wins. Everyone flourishes. Needs are met. People rise.

When we recreate this pattern through Mutual Success Teams, we're not experimenting. We're *repeating what worked*. And that means your success isn't just likely—it's *anchored in history.*

---

2. The Modern Application – Kingdom Economics in Real Life

Now, fast forward to today.

The world is still broken. Scarcity thinking still dominates. People still operate from fear, competition, and "me first" mentalities.

But the Kingdom hasn't changed. And neither has God's plan.

What we now call "Mutual Success Teams" is just the modern expression of that ancient model. It's Kingdom economics in action. It's Christians saying: *"Let's work together. Let's help each other. Let's build something where no one is left behind."*

And here's what that looks like in practice:

- One person creates a method for selling Scripture Decks at local events.
- Another finds success sharing them in homeschool communities.
- Someone else develops a strategy using social media and affiliate links.
- Each one documents what worked—and shares it.
- Now every new team member gets to *skip the guesswork* and start succeeding faster.

That's Kingdom economics. It's not just money—it's multiplied wisdom, multiplied opportunity, and multiplied care.

It's not every person for themselves—it's every person *for the whole*. And when that happens, we move from crisis to *consistency*.

That's what the modern church needs. And that's what you're helping build.

---

3. The Multiplication Principle – Success Repeats When It's Shared

Here's a truth that can change your entire mindset:

Success multiplies.

Not automatically—but intentionally. When you write down what worked, repeat it, and share it with others, your one-time win becomes a *reusable breakthrough*.

That's the Multiplication Principle. It's the foundation of discipleship, the pattern of effective business, and the strategy Jesus used to spread the Gospel: *"Go and make disciples... teaching them everything I have taught you."*

So here's what this means for your Mutual Success Team:

- When you succeed, *write it down.*
- Share it with others on your team.
- Let them try it.
- Celebrate when it works.
- Keep building forward—together.

This cycle turns your experience into a blueprint. It gives others a head start. And when they succeed, they'll do the same—building an upward spiral of learning, growing, and scaling.

The more you succeed *together*, the easier it becomes for the next person. And before long, what used to take months can be taught in minutes.

That's the power of shared success. That's the wisdom of the Multiplication Principle.

4. The Team Impact – From Scarcity to Abundance, Together

Let's say it clearly:

You're not in this alone.

That's not a slogan—it's a *reality*. When you're part of a Mutual Success Team, your burden is shared. Your growth is accelerated. Your mindset is constantly refreshed by the presence of others who believe in you.

And in that environment, *scarcity loses its grip.*

You stop wondering *"Can I do this?"* and start thinking *"How far can we take this?"*

You stop hoarding secrets, and start opening doors. You stop hiding your failures, and start transforming them into lessons that help everyone rise.

That's why this works.

Because success isn't just possible—it's *inevitable* in this model. With enough faith, support, and shared strategy, you *will* find a way. You *will* break through. And when you do, you won't stop. You'll multiply. You'll teach. You'll build the next team.

That's how we reach the goal again:

"There was no need among them."

That's what we're chasing. Not as a dream—but as a *deliverable*. A goal that can be reached. And you're holding the blueprint.

You're Part of Something Bigger—Much Bigger

This is bigger than decks. Bigger than business. Bigger than you.

This is about building the future of Christian provision. A future where local churches no longer struggle to fund their ministries. A future where families are free from paycheck-to-paycheck survival. A future where Christians aren't begging the world for opportunity—they're *building it themselves.*

And it starts with one step.

Your step.

Your willingness to succeed—not just for you, but for the people around you. For the people watching. For the people you haven't met yet, who are waiting for someone to show them what's possible.

You're not just creating income. You're modeling abundance. Kingdom abundance. And when you do that, *you change lives.*

The Mutual Success Solution Is the Path Forward

You've now seen both sides:

- The *reasons* you're set up to win (Chapter 9)
- The *biblical model* that guarantees long-term impact (this chapter)

Together, they form the **Mutual Success Solution**.

It's not just a clever idea. It's a tested, proven, scripture-backed way of building business, church, and legacy—all at once.

And now that you see it, the only thing left is to *step into it fully.*

Start sharing. Start collaborating. Start building your team.

And get ready to tell your story—because your breakthrough might be the next blueprint someone else is waiting for.

Part 2: The Stories – The Path Ahead: What Your Success Story Could Look Like

These are stories we created to show you possibilities. Each one may shed light on how you could succeed in this underdog of a Mutual Success Project — sharing 'Bible Scripture Playing Cards', a quiet revolution of insights and potential - that's just starting to ignite among Christians everywhere.

These profiles are strategic previews. Each story paints a picture of what it might look like for someone in your shoes to build purpose-driven income and impact. You'll meet relatable people: a mom at home, a college student online, a retired couple, a youth pastor, a quiet introvert—each navigating real-life challenges - while doing something meaningful.

You'll see how they get started, gain traction, and eventually build life-changing momentum—without needing to be sales experts or public speakers. The goal isn't hype. It's clarity. These examples are practical, plausible, and personal. They're here to help you see where you could fit — and how far you could go.

So read these stories as possibility. One of them may mirror your own path. One of them may unlock your "aha" moment. About a deck of Scripture cards and a Mutual Success Team committed to your success.

Chapter 11 – "The Stories": Inspiring You & Showing You the Potential

These are the glimpses of what can happen—when you say yes to purpose, and yes to starting small.

There is power in small things.

God has always delighted in using what the world overlooks. A mustard seed. A shepherd boy with a sling. Five loaves and two fish. A whisper instead of a shout. The Kingdom of Heaven doesn't need grandeur to produce greatness.

And now—maybe it starts with something as simple as a deck of cards.

A deck filled with scripture. Truth. Life. A small tool you can hold in your hands... that could unlock a bigger story in your life than you ever imagined.

This chapter introduces you to those stories.

They're not fiction. They're *possibility*. They're based on real situations, real lives, and real success paths that you or someone you know could step into *right now*.

These stories show the *power of starting small*—and the beauty of building something lasting. Something that serves others, glorifies God, and sets you up with both spiritual impact and financial overflow.

Each Story Is a Picture of Possibility

In the pages ahead, you'll meet people from different walks of life. A mom at home. A youth group leader. A retired couple. A college student. A pastor. An entrepreneur.

Each one faced different needs. Each one had different skills. But each one made the same decision:

"I want to do something that matters—and I want to start now."

They didn't wait for perfection. They didn't wait until they had all the answers. They took the first step—using a Scripture Deck and a few ideas—and everything began to change.

They shared their cards. They inspired others. They began making income. Then, they turned that income into *ongoing cash flow.* Permanent financial traction, built on something meaningful, spiritual, and simple.

That's the potential here.

These aren't complicated startup stories. They're everyday believers stepping into Kingdom momentum, *together.*

This Isn't Sales—It's Seed Planting

You don't need to be a public speaker.

You don't need a background in business.

You just need a heart that wants to help—and a willingness to move.

That's what these stories illustrate: how sharing a Scripture Deck can naturally spark conversations, open doors, and start a ripple effect that blesses everyone involved.

One conversation leads to another.

One gift opens someone's heart.

One deck plants one verse—and that verse changes a day... a life... a direction.

You're not just "distributing cards."

You're *distributing truth.*

And truth, when placed in someone's hands and heart, multiplies faster than anything else on Earth.

That's what makes this project so powerful.

It's not transactional. It's transformational.

These Stories Are Just the Beginning—Yours Is Next

As you read the examples in the next few chapters, see them as mirrors. Not blueprints to copy perfectly—but *models to learn from*.

Ask yourself:

- "What do I connect with in this story?"
- "What would this look like in *my* life?"
- "What's one idea I could borrow, adapt, or try?"

Because the real point isn't what they did.

It's that *they started.*

And so can you.

These stories show that it's possible—*realistically* and *reliably*—to use something small and simple like a deck of Scripture cards, and create:

- Encouragement for others
- Financial support for your family
- A team around you that believes in mutual success
- A long-term project that gives you peace and purpose

We believe that inside you is a story like this waiting to be written.

It won't look identical. It will be *yours.*

But it will begin with the same spark: one decision. One share. One act of faith.

And soon—you'll see it grow.

It's Your Turn to Discover What's Possible

The next seven chapters are more than profiles.

They are launching pads.

Each one shows how a different kind of person—with different circumstances and different gifts—found their fit, found their method, and found a path to purpose-filled income and spiritual impact.

Read them with expectation.

Read them with curiosity.

Read them asking, *"Could this be me?"*

And then answer: *Yes. If I'm willing to try. If I'm willing to grow. If I'm willing to believe God can use something small to do something extraordinary.*

Because He can. He will.

And your Mutual Success Team is here to help.

Let these stories show you what's possible.

Because when it comes to using your gifts for God, encouraging others, and building lasting income...

You are next.

Chapter 12 – "The Stories" - The Mom at Home

She didn't need a career shift—just a way to make a difference between nap time and Bible study.

"I wanted something real—but it had to fit my life."

That was her thought. Simple. Honest. And for years, unmet.

She wasn't looking to "build a business." She was raising three kids. She had laundry to fold, meals to make, homeschooling to plan, and a house to keep from collapsing. But in the quiet hours—when everyone was asleep and she had five minutes to herself—something stirred.

"Lord, I want to be used. I want to help people. I want to support our family, even just a little—but I don't want to sacrifice my calling as a mom to do it."

She looked at side hustles. She looked at Etsy shops. She even tried one of those direct sales things. Nothing fit.

Then a friend from church handed her a deck of Scripture Cards.

"They're beautiful," she said, flipping through them at the kitchen table that night. "And simple. And fun. And filled with the Word."

She felt it instantly: *this could work.*

Not just as a product—but as a purpose.

She Started with Her Circle

She didn't post to the world. She texted five women in her Bible study group.

"Hey! I've been using these Scripture Cards to keep my mind focused on the Lord during the day—especially in the crazy moments. Just thought I'd share. They've really helped."

The next day, one replied: "I NEED THESE. Where'd you get them?"

Then another: "Can I get a set for my daughter too?"

She ordered 10 decks. She gave a few away. She sold the rest without trying.

It was honest. Casual. Unforced. She wasn't "pitching"—she was helping.

That's when she realized: *I can do this in the margins of my day.*

She created a small system: while her kids napped or played, she messaged people she knew—friends from old churches, relatives, other moms. No scripts. Just real conversations.

The sales added up. So did the joy.

Her Life Didn't Change—But Her Confidence Did

She didn't stop being a mom. She didn't shift her identity. She simply added a new rhythm: *ministry through sharing*.

And her income? It started covering groceries. Then a car payment. Then a weekend away with her husband—paid for, without guilt.

But more than that, it gave her a new sense of *authority*.

She felt like she was multiplying the Word.

Not preaching.

Not teaching.

Just planting.

One deck at a time.

She's Building a Team Now

A few of the moms she shared with asked, *"Can I do this too?"*

She said yes.

She showed them how she did it: who she messaged, what she said, where she ordered.

She kept it simple.

And that simplicity turned into her first *Mutual Success Team.*

Now, she mentors three other women. They talk weekly. They pray. They share what's working. They celebrate each other's wins.

She never expected to lead. But now she is—quietly, steadily, faithfully.

And her story is multiplying.

Could This Be You?

You don't need a giant platform. You don't need a marketing degree. You just need *your real life*, and a desire to help others encounter God's Word in a simple way.

This mom didn't wait for perfect timing. She just started. And now she's seeing the fruit—not just in finances, but in *purpose*.

So if you're a mom at home—or anyone balancing a full life—let her story remind you:

You don't have to change your whole life to change someone else's.

You just have to share what's already in your hands.

Chapter 13 – "The Stories" - The Youth Group Leader

He wanted something that discipled his teens—without losing their attention.

"I'm tired of giving them hype with no depth."

That's what he told his pastor. And he meant it.

He had been leading the youth group at his church for three years. He loved it—but he felt stuck. Every week, he worked hard to make the lesson engaging. He used games, social media, lights, food—whatever he could to hold their focus. But after every Wednesday night, he asked the same quiet question:

"Are they actually getting it?"

He didn't want entertainment. He wanted transformation.

He wanted these teens to *own their faith*, not just visit it on youth night.

And then, one day, a ministry friend handed him a Scripture Deck.

At first, he didn't think much of it. A deck of cards? Nice, but probably a novelty.

Then he looked closer.

Each card had a verse. A theme. An application point.

Simple. Scriptural. Sharable.

He saw the potential instantly.

"What if this became part of discipleship?"

That next week, he handed a card to every student as they walked in.

No lecture. Just the card.

Some stuffed it in their pocket. A few read it right away. One kid said, "Wait—this is actually good."

He started using a card each week as part of the lesson. One week, the theme was identity. The next, fear. Then purpose. Then faith.

The cards gave him a structure—and gave the teens something to hold.

And slowly, things changed.

The students started *expecting* the cards. They asked questions. They quoted verses back. Some even began collecting them in their Bibles like bookmarks of breakthrough.

That's when it clicked.

He wasn't just running youth group anymore.

He was planting seeds.

From Tool to Team

As the students engaged, parents began to notice.

One mom said, "My son came home and read me his card out loud. That's never happened before."

Another asked if she could buy a deck for her daughter.

So he ordered more.

Then he made a few available after service.

Then someone asked, *"Can I help you sell these at my church too?"*

Without planning it, he was leading a Mutual Success Team.

Not just for money—but for mission.

He used the funds to offset costs for youth events. He gave decks to new students. He let the teens help design conversation starters around the verses.

Discipleship got deeper—and the Word became visible, personal, and portable.

He Didn't Need a New Curriculum—He Needed a Tool That Worked

This youth pastor didn't need to reinvent the wheel. He just needed something that made faith stick—and spread.

The Scripture Decks did both.

They sparked connection.

They built culture.

They made the Word of God the center—without making it feel like homework.

Now, he sees his role differently.

He's not just teaching kids—he's equipping them.

And he's inviting others to do the same.

Could This Be You?

If you work with teens, you know the challenge: they're over-stimulated, over-scheduled, and often spiritually undernourished.

This story proves you don't need to fight for attention.

You just need to place the Word where it can *work*.

Maybe your first step is handing out a single card. Maybe it's inviting your youth team to start a Mutual Success Project together.

Whatever it looks like, remember: you're not just leading a group.

You're leading *a generation*.

And a single card can start a revival in someone's story.

Chapter 14 – "The Stories" - The Retired Couple at a Farmer's Market

They weren't looking for something new. But God had one more assignment—and it came with a folding table.

"We just wanted to do something together—and make it count."

They had entered retirement with peace in their hearts. After decades of work, ministry, and raising a family, they were finally able to slow down. No more deadlines. No more commutes. Just early coffee, porch conversations, and the joy of unhurried mornings.

But after a while, they felt it: that gentle stirring that says, *"You're not done yet."*

They didn't want to go back to the grind. But they did want to *give back*. Something low-pressure. Something fun. Something that honored the Lord—and each other.

That's when a friend mentioned a local farmer's market booth where vendors could sell homemade products, crafts, and Christian items.

They had nothing to sell... yet.

But then she remembered the Scripture Decks.

They had picked up a set from a friend's church a few months earlier. Every morning, they read one together during breakfast. It became a sweet ritual. A daily dose of encouragement that anchored them before the day began.

So she said, "What if we got a box of these and just... offered them?"

He smiled. "Let's try it."

They Started Small—with One Table and Two Chairs

The next weekend, they set up their table. A small sign. A few display stands. A tablecloth she found in the back of the linen closet.

They didn't pitch. They didn't pressure. They just *talked*.

People stopped. Flipped through the cards. Smiled.

One woman said, "These are so uplifting. My sister just got diagnosed—I think she'd love these."

Another said, "I haven't read my Bible in years... but this verse really got me."

And one man stood silently at the table, reading a card that said, *"Come to Me, all who are weary..."*

He didn't speak. He just nodded. And walked away with a deck.

That night, the couple sat in the living room, grateful and a little stunned.

"We didn't just sell," he said. "We *ministered*."

Ministry in Retirement—And Income Too

Over the next few weeks, they kept going. One Saturday at a time. One conversation at a time.

Some weekends were slow. Some were surprising. But each time, they came home with stories—and income.

It wasn't about making a fortune. It was about making a *difference*—and about having something they could do *together*.

They called it their "scripture stand." And every Saturday, people returned—some just to say thank you, others to buy more decks for friends and family.

They realized something powerful: this wasn't just a product. It was a *touchpoint*. A chance to bring God's Word into places where it usually wasn't—like a dusty market corner between fresh honey and hand-poured candles.

They had found their post-retirement assignment. Not busywork. Not burnout.

Just purpose. Shared.

They Became Quiet Catalysts

Soon, a younger couple from their church asked how they could do the same thing. The retired couple shared everything they had learned: how to set up the booth, what signage worked, which questions sparked conversations.

They didn't gatekeep. They *gave*.

And that's when their booth became a *Mutual Success Team*.

Now, they weren't just serving customers. They were mentoring others. Guiding them. Praying with them. Multiplying what God had started with a single table and two willing hearts.

They said it best:

"This isn't a side hustle. This is seed sowing. And retirement isn't the end—it's just a new field to work in."

Could This Be You?

If you're retired—or approaching that season—you don't have to start big. You don't even need a business background.

You just need a table. A little space. And a willingness to share what's blessed you.

Farmer's markets. Craft fairs. Church lobbies. Community gatherings. These are fertile grounds for faith—if you're willing to show up.

Like this couple, your life may already be full. But there's still room for one more assignment. One more calling. One more small act of obedience that opens big doors.

You don't need pressure.

You need *purpose*.

And you already have it—in your heart and in your hands.

Chapter 15 – "The Stories" - The College Student Online

He needed tuition money—but he wanted something more meaningful than delivering food or going into debt.

"I didn't want to waste four years just surviving."

That was the thought that ran through his mind as he sat in his dorm room, staring at his laptop.

He had just come back from a part-time job interview at a local fast-food chain. It was decent money, but something in his spirit said, *"Not this. Not for four years. There has to be something else."*

His schedule was packed—classes, labs, study sessions. He was trying to balance being a full-time student and staying faithful in his walk with God. But the financial pressure was real. Rent. Books. Food. Gas. And tuition... always looming in the background.

He didn't want to ask his parents for more help. He didn't want to borrow from the government again.

So he started praying: *"Lord, show me something I can do—something I won't regret. Something that lets me stay focused on You."*

That night, while scrolling Instagram, he saw someone post a picture of a Scripture Card laid out next to a journal.

The caption was simple: *"This card showed up exactly when I needed it. Love how God speaks through His Word!"*

He followed the link. And fifteen minutes later, he ordered his first deck.

He Started with One Post

He didn't think of it as a business. He just loved the design. The simplicity. The daily encouragement.

So he snapped a photo. Shared how he was using the cards to start his day. Tagged the brand. And kept it moving.

But then something happened.

A classmate commented: "Wait, where did you get these?"

Another messaged him privately: "I've been looking for something like this for my morning routine. Send me the link?"

So he shared it. Then made a short TikTok about how he pulls a card every morning and prays through the verse. Nothing flashy—just honest.

The next week, he got three messages from people who had bought decks using his link.

Then five more.

Then someone asked, *"Can I buy one from you directly?"*

It Turned Into a Real Income Stream—Faster Than He Expected

He started ordering a few decks at a time. He kept one or two in his backpack. He'd give them to people in his Bible study or offer them on campus between classes.

But most of his impact came from online.
Short videos. Reels. Posts with a verse and a reflection.
Sometimes just a picture of the card and a question like, *"Which verse is holding you up right now?"*

It wasn't salesy. It was soulful.

And that's what made it work.

In his third month, he earned more from deck sales and referrals than he would have made working 12 hours a week at the burger place.

But more than that, he started hearing stories.

People messaging him, thanking him for the encouragement. Friends sharing how the cards helped them reconnect with God. One person even said, "I got a deck for my cousin who just came out of rehab. It's been a lifeline for her."

He realized: *This isn't just a product. This is ministry disguised as content.*

He's Not Just a Student Anymore—He's a Leader Online

He didn't set out to be an influencer. But now he's leading a small online Mutual Success Team made up of other students, creatives, and faith-focused young adults who want to do something that matters.

He shows them what's working. What to post. How to link. How to keep it authentic.

They're learning together. Growing together. Earning together.

And through it all, he's stayed focused. His grades are strong. His relationship with God is stronger. And he's no longer anxious about next semester's bills.

Because he's building something that works—in the real world and the Kingdom.

Could This Be You?

If you're a student—or anyone navigating a busy, tech-connected life—this might be your on-ramp.

You don't need a platform. You need a story. A rhythm. A reason to post with purpose.

And when the Word of God is your message, people will respond.

Start small. Post a verse. Share your quiet time. Tell the truth.

And watch what happens.

Because when you combine faith with a tool that makes an impact, you don't just earn income—you make disciples.

And that's a kind of success the world can't cancel.

Chapter 16 – "The Stories" - The Pastor Funding Their Next Project

They had the vision. They had the people. They just needed a sustainable way to fund what God was calling them to build.

"I'm not asking for luxury—I'm asking for enough."

That was the pastor's prayer. Not for a mansion. Not for a jet. Just enough to fund what God had laid on his heart. The vision was clear: launch a new outreach program, open a resource center for struggling families, and bring on a part-time staff member to disciple youth.

The need was great. The people were willing. The ideas were ready.

But the funds… weren't there.

Tithes covered the basics. Rent. Utilities. A modest honorarium. But anything beyond that—especially the kind of Kingdom projects that served the community—was always a stretch. And asking the same faithful members to "dig deeper" again and again felt exhausting.

"I want to stop begging and start building," he told his wife one night.

That's when he remembered something someone had handed him after a conference—a Scripture Deck.

It had been sitting on his bookshelf for months.

He picked it up.

And this time, he didn't just see a deck of cards.

He saw *a way forward.*

He Saw the Deck as More Than a Devotional—He Saw It as a Funding Tool

That week, he brought the deck to his staff meeting.

He placed it in the center of the table and said, "What if this became our bridge?"

He explained how it worked. How simple it was. How churches and individuals could use them to encourage others—and how, when shared strategically, they could also generate income.

"Not from manipulation," he said. "From multiplication."

The team caught the vision.

They ordered 50 decks. They didn't push them during service. They simply made them available at the info table. Added a note in the bulletin. Told a few testimonies about how the cards were helping people stay rooted in the Word.

People responded.

The first Sunday, 12 decks were picked up. The next, 20. One woman came back and bought three more—one for each of her grown kids.

Within three weeks, they had made enough to cover printing costs and raise money toward the youth outreach program.

More importantly, something shifted.

The church wasn't just asking for help anymore.

They were *offering something that helped others.*

The Pastor Shared the Vision—and the Church Joined the Mission

Soon, a few members came forward: "Can I help promote these in my business?" "Could I take a box to my cousin's church?" "I'm part of a women's fellowship—can we offer these at our retreat?"

The answer was yes.

The pastor wasn't just leading a congregation now. He was equipping a Mutual Success Team.

He created a shared document outlining what had worked—how they positioned the decks, what kind of language resonated, how to cast the vision without pressure. The church's admin team helped track income. One tech-savvy member built a simple ordering page.

They weren't becoming a merchandise ministry.

They were becoming a *resource hub.*

And the funds? They kept coming.

Enough to launch the outreach.

Enough to bring on a part-time staffer.

Enough to fund the *next* God-given idea.

He Still Preaches—But Now He Builds, Too

Nothing changed about his calling. He still preached on Sundays. Still visited hospitals. Still led prayer meetings.

But something had *expanded.*

He wasn't stuck in the cycle of "vision without provision." He had found a way to let the Word of God work in more than one way: spiritually and practically.

He said it like this:

"These cards don't just encourage people—they empower churches."

And now, he's helping other pastors do the same.

He's hosting training sessions. Sharing the template. Showing them how to use Scripture Decks to serve their people and fund their mission—with dignity, clarity, and joy.

Could This Be You?

If you're a pastor—or someone serving in ministry—you don't have to stay stuck between God's calling and man's limitations.

There is a way to fund what God gave you.

You don't need to chase gimmicks. You don't need to drain your people.

You just need a product that carries *both power and purpose.*

And that's exactly what this is.

A tool. A seed. A solution.

And the next step in your ministry's journey to *overflow.*

Chapter 17 – "The Stories" - The Entrepreneur Building Recurring Cash Flow

He didn't need a new idea—he needed a system that could scale with heart and produce with consistency.

"I've built things before. I wanted to build something I didn't have to chase."

He was no stranger to business. In fact, by most accounts, he was successful.

Over the years, he had launched three companies. One failed fast. One limped along. One actually worked—but only when he worked *nonstop*. And that was the problem.

He was tired.

Not tired of creating—tired of maintaining. Tired of chasing leads. Tired of watching income spike one month and fall the next. Tired of always having to *be on* just to keep things moving.

He wanted recurring revenue—*stable, ethical, low-friction income* that didn't demand every waking hour.

But even more than that... he wanted mission.

He wanted to build something he could stand behind. Something that didn't just make money, but made a difference. Something that could be passed on, shared, and scaled—*without losing his soul.*

He prayed: *"Lord, show me something I can build once—and use to bless others long after."*

That's when a friend in ministry told him about Scripture Decks.

He was intrigued.

But when he saw the Mutual Success Team model?

He was *in.*

He Didn't Need to Reinvent—He Just Needed to Plug In

As an entrepreneur, he immediately saw what others didn't.

"This is a turnkey product," he said. "Low overhead, zero need for a warehouse, no complicated sales process. And the emotional impact is instant. That's rare."

He ordered a few decks. Created a simple landing page. Recorded a short video—just him, sharing what he liked about the cards and how they helped keep him grounded in the Word while running his business.

Within the first 10 days, he had 17 orders.

More importantly, 9 of those customers messaged him.

They weren't just buyers. They were *grateful.*

They told him how the decks helped them start their day better. How their kids had started reading scripture again. One said she felt "like she had something holy in her purse."

He smiled. *"That's the difference,"* he thought. *"That's what most businesses miss."*

He Created a Funnel That Worked While He Slept

True to his entrepreneur mindset, he optimized quickly.

He linked the decks to his existing email list of faith-minded professionals. He built an automated follow-up that asked one simple question: *"Would you like to sell these too?"*

Some said yes.

He showed them how.

Within six weeks, he had 11 people in his downline. Not hard sellers. Not "sales reps." Just real people who had used the product and wanted to share it.

Each one used a different method. Some on Instagram. Others through small events. A few just texted friends. But together? They started generating real numbers.

The best part?

He didn't have to micromanage them.

He mentored. He checked in. He celebrated. But the engine ran without him having to be everywhere at once.

And just like that, the recurring cash flow began.

He Shifted from Earning to Empowering

At first, it was just about the income.

Then, it became about *the people.*

One woman on his team used her sales to pay for her son's braces. Another used hers to support a missionary friend overseas. One man told him, "This is the first time I've made money doing something that feels like ministry."

That's when he realized: *"I'm not just earning—I'm empowering."*

And that's when his leadership deepened.

He started refining his onboarding guide. He gave his team templated emails, photos, and scripts they could personalize. He hosted monthly Zoom calls to answer questions, pray together, and strategize.

The more he gave, the more they grew.

And the more they grew, the more stable his income became.

Now, the system he built once keeps producing every single month.

No burnout. No grind.

Just *good fruit.*

Could This Be You?

If you're an entrepreneur—or just someone who thinks in systems and scale—this model is your match.

You don't need to invent a product. You don't need to do it all alone. You don't even need a massive platform.

You just need clarity.

You need a product with meaning. A system that works. A team that multiplies. And a mission that lasts.

This is recurring revenue that flows through *people and purpose.*

And it starts the moment you decide to build something *bigger than yourself.*

Part 3: The Deck – Card Business System Explained

Before you launch your business, you need to understand how everything works. This part of the book is where we lay out the full system behind Christian Decks—so you're not guessing, you're growing.

You'll learn the psychology behind the cards, the simplicity of the $20 price point, and why this product sells itself—especially when shared in a relationship-centered way. We'll cover who buys them, how they're used, and how the profit system creates success for everyone involved.

We'll also introduce a brand-new product: the "Mutual Success Team" Deck. This unique set of 52 cards is designed around four biblical themes—Community, Wealth Building, Leadership, and Success. It's made for discipleship, devotion, and team development all in one.

By the end of this section, you'll have clarity. You'll know how to explain, share, and sell with confidence. You won't just be holding cards. You'll be holding the blueprint for your business and the seed of something that could grow beyond what you imagined.

Chapter 18 – How the Cards Work: Scripture + Relationship Building

They're not just cards. They're conversation starters. Faith igniters. Bridges between people and the Word.

What if one verse could start something deeper?

That's what makes Scripture Decks so unique. They don't preach. They *prompt*. They don't pressure. They *open*. They create a moment—sometimes quiet, sometimes surprising—where God's truth can enter the room in a way that feels personal, timely, and real.

The idea is simple: each deck contains 52 beautifully designed cards. On the front: a powerful scripture. On the back: a short phrase or application prompt. You can use them alone or with others. You can draw one randomly each day or pick one for a theme or situation.

But the real beauty? These cards don't just build up the individual. They *build relationships.*

When shared, they open doors—between friends, families, church groups, or even total strangers. They're the perfect excuse to say something meaningful. They help people start spiritual conversations that don't feel awkward or forced.

And in a world filled with shallow talk, these cards go straight to the heart—gently, but powerfully.

They're Designed to Do More Than Encourage You

Yes, the cards are encouraging. They're great for personal devotions, quiet time, and morning routines.

But their deeper purpose is *connection*—with God and with others.

Here's how:

- **They give you language.** Not everyone knows how to start a faith conversation. These cards do it for you.
- **They feel safe.** You're not handing someone a heavy theological tract—you're handing them a verse and a blessing.
- **They invite participation.** You can ask, "Which verse speaks to you today?" and suddenly, a meaningful conversation begins.
- **They stir memory and truth.** People often say, "I needed this exact verse today." The Holy Spirit knows what to highlight.

They're more than tools. They're *triggers for transformation*.

And when used consistently—in a family, a team, a church, or a business—they help create a shared spiritual atmosphere that keeps everyone focused on truth.

They Make Faith Visible, Portable, and Tangible

One of the greatest challenges in today's world is staying spiritually focused in everyday life. Our phones distract us. Our schedules rush us. Our minds wander.

But when the Word is on the table, on the dashboard, on the kitchen counter—it *re-centers us.*

These decks bring scripture into the physical world. They make it *visible.* Something you can hold. Something you can gift. Something that doesn't need Wi-Fi or a screen.

People use them:

- During daily prayer time
- At dinner with family
- In small group discussions
- At church welcome tables
- As gifts to visitors or volunteers
- As memory verses for kids or youth
- In counseling and mentorship settings

They meet people where they are—with truth that fits in the palm of your hand.

And in doing that, they shift the culture of a room—from distracted to *devoted.*

They Create a Culture of Sharing—Not Selling

Another thing that sets Scripture Decks apart is how naturally they're shared.

You're not selling someone a product in the traditional sense. You're *offering something that helped you*. You're saying, "Here's a verse that blessed me today—maybe it'll speak to you, too."

That exchange creates trust. And that trust builds relationships.

One of the most beautiful side effects of this is that Scripture Decks often get passed along long before a sale ever happens. People give one away. Then that person buys their own. Then *they* give one away.

The Word spreads, and so does the opportunity.

That's why these decks work so well inside a Mutual Success Team. Because the goal isn't just to build a customer base—it's to build a *faith community.*

A culture of scripture-sharing.

A circle of Kingdom conversations.

A rhythm of encouragement that keeps reaching.

This Is Relationship Evangelism at Its Best

The power of the Gospel is always best delivered in *relationship*. People listen when they trust. They open up when they feel seen.

And that's what a Scripture Deck does—it meets someone in the flow of their life with a word that invites God into the moment.

You don't need to preach. You don't need to explain everything. You just need to offer a verse.

Let the Word do what it always does: comfort, challenge, inspire, and draw.

And as the conversations flow, the relationships deepen.

That's not just business growth.

That's *discipleship.*

Chapter 19 – The Pricing Strategy: Why $20 Works Perfectly

It's not just a price tag. It's a doorway—to value, dignity, and sustainable impact.

"Should I really charge for something with scripture on it?"

That's the question many Christians ask when they first begin.

And it's a good question—one rooted in integrity and spiritual caution. We never want to commercialize the Word of God. We never want to turn ministry into manipulation.

But here's the truth: *pricing isn't about greed—it's about stewardship.*

The $20 price point for Scripture Decks wasn't chosen randomly. It's intentional. It creates space for healthy business growth, fair compensation, generous sharing, and sustainable impact.

This chapter will show you why that price isn't just acceptable—it's *ideal*. It respects the value of the product, honors the mission behind it, and creates the kind of ecosystem that allows everyone to win—buyers, sellers, and those who receive.

Because when you understand the pricing strategy, you stop feeling awkward about it—and start standing confidently behind what you're offering.

---

1. It's Affordable—but Valuable

In today's world, $20 is accessible. It's not cheap—but it's not expensive either. It falls into that sweet spot: high enough to communicate value, low enough to feel like a reasonable impulse purchase.

You can compare it to:

- A lunch date
- A movie ticket with snacks
- A modest gift for a coworker or teacher

People *spend* $20 all the time without thinking.

The difference is, when they spend $20 on a Scripture Deck, they're not buying a fleeting experience. They're buying a tool they can use *over and over.* Something that blesses them daily. Something that lasts.

The perceived value is strong.

And that's why customers don't just buy—they come back. They gift it. They recommend it.

Because it *feels worth it.*

---

2. It Creates Meaningful Profit—for You and Your Team

Let's be honest: a $5 product can't support a business. Not sustainably.

And a $50 product can feel too risky for a new customer.

But $20? It generates meaningful income—*without scaring people off.*

For every deck sold at $20, there's room for $10 to $15 in profit, depending on your cost structure and how you order or distribute. That's a strong margin. One that allows you to:

- Cover costs
- Reinvest
- Give generously
- Support your family
- Build a team

And when your team grows, each person benefits. The $20 price point allows for group-based success. It creates enough margin that you can *bless others* while still earning yourself.

That's not just smart—it's *Kingdom-minded.*

---

3. It Respects the Craft

Each Scripture Deck is thoughtfully designed. It's not a PDF download or a throwaway trinket. It's high-quality. Printed. Packaged. Portable.

And it's filled with the most powerful words in existence.

If we truly believe in the product, we should *price it like we believe in it.*

Underpricing communicates "this doesn't matter." Overpricing communicates "this is only for the elite."

But $20 says: "This is beautiful. Useful. Spiritual. And you can access it today."

It dignifies the product.

It honors the effort that went into creating it.

And it invites people to invest—emotionally and financially—in something that will bless their lives.

---

4. It Fuels Generosity Without Creating Loss

Want to give a deck away? Great.

Because the $20 model *allows for that.*

You can afford to donate one deck for every five you sell—and still remain profitable. You can bless a church leader. Gift a friend. Surprise a customer. Fund a missions trip. Run a "buy one, give one" promo.

Generosity isn't a subtraction. It becomes *part of the system.*

That's what makes this pricing strategy so powerful—it keeps the mission *and* the money moving forward, without guilt or imbalance.

You're not stuck between "profit or purpose."

You get *both.*

---

5. It Builds a Sustainable Future—for You and for Others

Most income models burn out because they rely on volume without margin.

The $20 strategy flips that.

You don't need to move thousands of units. Just a few consistent ones each week can create real momentum.

Let's break it down:

- Sell 5 decks/week = $50–75 profit
- Sell 20 decks/month = $200–100+ side income
- Build a team of 5 doing the same = $1,000+ flowing through your network
- Scale up with digital outreach or events = $2,000–$5,000+ potential

All from a product that people *want, use,* and *talk about.*

That's not just sustainability. That's *scalability.*

And it's possible because the pricing is smart, balanced, and purposeful.

Price Is Part of the Mission

Never forget this: you're not just selling cards.

You're offering encouragement, empowerment, and scripture—packaged in a way that's easy to receive.

The $20 price tag simply makes that possible.

It creates room for impact *and* income.

It keeps things simple *and* strong.

It builds a foundation others can duplicate—without risk, without burnout, and without apology.

So own it. Share it confidently.

Because when someone asks, *"Why $20?"*

You can smile and say, *"Because that's what makes this sustainable—for all of us."*

Chapter 20 – The Target Market: Who Buys (Everyone Needs Encouragement)

This isn't a niche product—it's a heart product. And the audience is everywhere.

"Who would actually want to buy Scripture Cards?"

It's a fair question—and one of the first people ask before starting. They wonder if it's "too Christian," "too simple," "too niche." But the answer is always bigger than expected:

Almost everyone.

Why? Because **everyone needs encouragement.**

We live in a world that is flooded with information and starving for truth. People scroll endlessly but rarely feel fed. They see thousands of messages a day—but few offer hope, clarity, or peace.

That's where Scripture Decks come in. They cut through the noise. They aren't loud, but they speak loud enough. They don't preach—but they *reach.*

This chapter will walk you through the real-world audiences—your true target market—who are not only willing to buy these decks, but *eager* to find something like this. You won't need to pressure. You just need to *present*. Because what you're offering is rare, refreshing, and relevant.

---

1. Christians of All Denominations

This is the obvious one—but don't underestimate its power.

Christians across all traditions—Protestant, Catholic, Pentecostal, Baptist, non-denominational—*love the Word of God.* And Scripture Decks are an easy, accessible way to engage with it.

These buyers use the decks for:

- Daily devotionals
- Gifts for family and friends
- Bible studies and small groups
- Sermon illustrations
- Sunday school and youth group tools

They're often the first to understand the value. But once they do, they're also the *first to spread the word.*

You're not introducing something strange. You're offering something *familiar and useful*—just in a better format.

---

2. Parents and Families

Parents are constantly looking for ways to keep faith in the home—without fighting attention spans.

Scripture Decks solve that.

They're visual, portable, and engaging. Parents use them at dinner, bedtime, in the car, or as part of homeschool routines. Kids flip through them on their own. Teens keep a favorite card in their backpack. Spouses pick one to start their morning prayer together.

It's spiritual connection *without a long time commitment*.

And because the decks are durable and beautiful, they make *great gifts* for holidays, birthdays, and milestones.

You're not just selling to one person—you're often selling to a *whole household.*

---

3. Gift Buyers and Givers

One of the biggest drivers of Scripture Deck sales is gifting.

These cards make the perfect:

- Encouragement gift
- "Thinking of you" gesture
- Welcome basket addition
- Thank-you to volunteers
- Conference giveaway
- Stocking stuffer
- Mother's Day or Father's Day token
- Bereavement gift or recovery support

Because they're affordable, spiritual, and heartfelt, they check every box. People *want* to give something that uplifts—and this is exactly that.

Many customers don't even buy for themselves first—they buy to bless someone else. That means you're offering a product that travels farther than the initial sale.

The reach is multiplied by the *intention* behind it.

---

4. Church Leaders and Ministries

Pastors, small group leaders, prayer team coordinators, and ministry volunteers are always searching for tools to help disciple, train, and encourage others.

When they see these cards, they immediately think:

- "I could use this in my class."
- "I'd love to give one to every new visitor."
- "Our prayer team would love these."
- "This would fit our next women's retreat."

Churches love that these are versatile: not preachy, but powerful. Not heavy, but holy.

And once a leader sees how effective they are, they often *buy in bulk.*

This opens doors for partnerships, repeat orders, and entire-team Mutual Success opportunities.

---

5. People Outside the Church Who Still Want Encouragement

Here's the surprise: your target market isn't limited to active churchgoers.

Many people who aren't currently in church—or haven't been in years—still crave truth. They're not anti-God. They're just tired of religion that feels irrelevant.

But Scripture? That still speaks.

When they see a verse that hits home, they pause.

That's why these decks also resonate with:

- Co-workers in crisis

- Friends going through loss
- People exploring faith
- Those in recovery communities
- Teachers, nurses, caregivers, and more

You're not preaching at them. You're offering a *gentle spark*. And often, that opens up deeper conversation and interest.

Don't count anyone out.

You're Not Just Selling—You're Placing Hope Where It's Needed Most

Your target market isn't just defined by faith background. It's defined by *emotional need.*

Who needs peace?

Who needs clarity?

Who's navigating uncertainty?

Who's trying to rebuild their faith?

Answer: just about everyone.

Scripture Decks are the perfect blend of accessible truth and relational delivery. And that makes them relevant in nearly *any setting.*

So don't overthink your audience.

Think of one person who could use a lift.
Start there.

Because the moment they feel the impact of just one verse—your "market" becomes a *ministry.*

Chapter 21 – The Selling Process: Natural, Relationship-Based Approach

You're not pitching. You're sharing. That's what makes it work—and what makes it feel right.

"I'm not a salesperson."

If you've ever said that, you're not alone. In fact, it's one of the most common things we hear from people starting out.

But the good news is—you don't need to be.

Because selling Scripture Decks isn't about crafting the perfect pitch. It's not about memorizing a script, creating urgency, or mastering the art of closing a deal.

It's about *building connection*.

You're not convincing someone to buy something they don't want. You're offering something they probably already need—

encouragement, clarity, and a fresh way to engage with God's Word.

That's why this chapter is all about the natural, relationship-based approach. It works for moms, pastors, introverts, entrepreneurs, and everyday believers. It feels comfortable, kind, and aligned with your values.

It's selling without pressure. Business without burnout. Ministry *through* conversation.

Let's walk through what it looks like.

---

1. Start With What's Real for You

Before you ever talk to someone else about the product, start with this question:

How has this helped me?

That's your foundation. Because people don't need a polished pitch—they want your *personal experience.*

Did a certain verse speak to you this week? Did the cards help you feel more connected to God? Did a friend respond emotionally when you gifted them a deck?

That's what you share.

You can say:

- "This helped me stay grounded this week."
- "I've been using these with my kids during breakfast."
- "A friend gave me this, and it's become a part of my morning routine."

No exaggeration. No pressure. Just your honest testimony.

And here's the beautiful thing—your story sells.

---

2. Focus on Conversations, Not Conversions

You're not here to *convert* someone into a customer. You're here to *connect.*

Most people aren't ready to buy the first time they hear about something. That's okay. Don't force it. Just talk. Ask questions. Listen.

Let the Scripture Deck be part of the relationship—not the center of it.

The goal of a natural, relationship-based approach is this:

- Build trust
- Offer value
- Let the person decide

This takes the pressure off *you*—and makes it easier for *them* to say yes when the time is right.

Because people don't buy when they feel pushed.

They buy when they feel *seen*.

---

3. Share Through the Channels You Already Use

You don't need a new persona or a new platform.

Just use what's already in front of you.

- **Text a friend:** "Hey! Thought of you when I saw this verse today—wanted to share the card I pulled this morning."
- **Post online:** A quick photo, a 1-sentence reflection, and a link.
- **In-person moments:** At church, in a small group, over coffee. Keep a few decks with you to hand out or show.
- **Emails and group messages:** Mention how the cards are helping you and include a way for others to get them.

The more casual it feels, the better it works.

Because you're not "selling." You're *inviting.* You're showing something valuable—and letting people come closer at their own pace.

---

4. Ask the Right Questions

Sometimes the best way to offer something isn't to *explain* it—it's to *ask* something meaningful.

Try questions like:

- "What's one verse that's helped you recently?"
- "Do you have a daily devotional rhythm that works for you?"
- "Have you seen these Scripture Decks? I've been using them—they're such a blessing."

Questions spark dialogue. Dialogue leads to curiosity. And curiosity opens doors.

People respond when they feel like it's about *them*, not just the product.

So become a question-asker.

It's the simplest way to serve—and one of the most effective ways to share.

---

5. Let the Product Speak for Itself

Once someone sees or holds a deck, the rest is easy.

The beauty, the scriptures, the simplicity—it speaks.

So whenever possible, put a deck in someone's hands. Or send a photo. Or let them read a few cards.

Your job is to *introduce the experience.*

The product will do the rest.

And if they're not ready today? No problem.

The seed is planted. Keep the relationship strong. Keep living what you share.

The harvest often comes later.

This Is Selling That Feels Like Serving

You're not chasing people. You're offering peace.

You're not managing leads. You're ministering encouragement.

You're not "getting people to buy." You're helping them *see the value* of something that could bless their lives deeply.

And in that space—sales happen. Naturally. Repeatedly. Joyfully.

So take the pressure off.

Lead with relationship.

Let trust do the talking.

And watch how God uses your heart—not your hustle—to grow something that truly lasts.

Chapter 22 – The Profit Structure: How Everyone Wins

When the system is built on mutual blessing, profit becomes more than income—it becomes impact.

"Can I actually earn from this... without compromising my values?"

It's the question most Christians ask when stepping into a business opportunity. They want to provide for their families, but they don't want to get caught in hype, pressure, or greed. They want something sustainable—*and sacred.*

That's where the profit structure behind Christian Decks stands apart.

This model isn't just profitable—it's *mutually profitable.* It's designed so that *everyone involved wins*—from the person using the deck for morning encouragement, to the one selling it at a church event, to the team leader who's helping others grow.

It's not "top-heavy." It's not performance-driven. It's not built on personality cults or manipulation.

It's built on **kingdom principles of stewardship, multiplication, and generosity.**

Let's break it down clearly—so you can understand how the money flows, why it works, and why it feels different (because it *is* different).

---

1. It Starts With a Strong Margin

Each Scripture Deck sells for around **$20**.

The wholesale cost to you (depending on your order size and printing method) typically ranges from **$4 to $8** per deck. That means you're earning anywhere from **$12 to $16 in profit per sale.**

That's significant.

It gives you margin—not just in your bank account, but in your energy. You don't need to sell 100 decks to see progress. You can sell five and feel momentum. Ten, and you're covering bills. Twenty or more, and you're building overflow.

This kind of profit margin means:

- You can give away a few decks without losing steam

- You can reinvest in your next order
- You can fund your family, your ministry, and your future

And all of it comes from a simple, meaningful product people *already want.*

---

2. You Can Build Recurring Revenue With Teams

The moment you start sharing your method with others—your income has the potential to become *recurring*.

Let's say you help five people begin their own small Scripture Deck outreach. You train them. Mentor them. You show them what's worked for you.

Each time they sell decks, they win. And when the structure is set up right, **you win too**—through commissions, overrides, or bonuses built into the system.

This is not multi-level hype.

It's *multiplication through mentorship*.

And that's a biblical principle.

Jesus multiplied Himself through twelve disciples. Paul trained Timothy. Every spiritual leader in scripture passed something on.

This system is no different.

You earn more—not by selling more yourself—but by helping others succeed.

That's not only financially smart. It's *deeply Kingdom-minded.*

---

3. The Buyer Wins—Because the Product Delivers Real Value

None of this would matter if the deck didn't work. But it does.

Every person who buys a Scripture Deck is receiving:

- 52 verses of truth and life
- A tool that strengthens their walk with God
- A devotional that's portable, giftable, and usable
- A product they're proud to share

That means every purchase is a blessing. Every transaction is a testimony. And every customer is *being served*—not just "sold to."

There's no guilt in earning when the product *gives more than it takes.*

That's what makes this model unique.

You're not extracting value.

You're *delivering it.*

And when customers feel that? They don't just buy—they *believe.*

---

4. The Team Member Wins—Because Growth Is Shared, Not Strained

In many traditional sales structures, the pressure is constant. Hit quotas. Compete with teammates. Perform or perish.

But Mutual Success Teams aren't built like that.

They're built on *shared strategy*, open communication, and celebration—not competition.

Each new team member wins by:

- Choosing the method that fits their life
- Getting mentoring and support (not pressure)
- Earning real profit without burnout
- Having their success *cheered*, not envied

You're not just building a sales force. You're building *a community.*

And that creates retention, joy, and sustainability.

It's not a race—it's a rhythm.

And everyone who joins feels that from day one.

---

5. The Kingdom Wins—Because the Mission Multiplies

Finally, let's talk about the most important win: *the Kingdom.*

Every deck sold sends the Word of God into someone's hand, home, or heart. Every card drawn could be the verse that changes a life. Every team that forms creates a hub of faith, provision, and outreach.

And every dollar earned is a dollar that can be used for good.

- Supporting missions
- Funding church projects
- Helping families in need
- Creating overflow so believers can give without fear

This is the kind of profit that doesn't just build lifestyles—it builds *legacy.*

Because when the Kingdom wins, the world gets changed.

Everyone Wins—And That's the Point

You win.
Your customer wins.
Your team wins.
Your church wins.
The Kingdom wins.

That's the profit structure. Simple. Ethical. Powerful.

So don't hesitate to step in. Don't feel guilty about earning. Don't question if this is "too good to be true."

Because when profit is built on purpose—*it's a gift.*

And it's yours to receive, multiply, and share.

Chapter 23 – Introducing: The "Mutual Success Team" Deck – How It Was Designed

Every card is a piece of your mission. Together, they build a spiritual blueprint for sustainable success.

This deck was built for more than inspiration. It was built for transformation—together.

When we designed the *Mutual Success Team* Scripture Deck, we weren't just choosing 52 random verses to uplift people. We were building a structure—a set of spiritual pillars to help you and your team *flourish together.*

Each card in this deck plays a specific role. Each scripture reinforces a truth essential to building a strong, sustainable, and spiritually aligned *Mutual Success Team*. That means these aren't just cards to be read—they're tools to *live by.*

They help you build teams with purpose.

Businesses with values.

Communities that care.

And they anchor everything in the Word of God.

So let's take a closer look at how this deck was designed, and why every suit carries a message that speaks directly into your team's journey.

Hearts: Community (13 cards)

Because no one builds alone—and no one should have to.

The suit of **Hearts** was crafted to anchor your team in *relational strength*. These verses speak to unity, connection, and shared burdens—the kind of community that turns business partnerships into spiritual family.

Key Scriptures include:

- **Acts 4:32–35** – *"All the believers were one in heart and mind... there were no needy persons among them."*
- **1 Corinthians 12:26** – *"If one suffers, all suffer; if one rejoices, all rejoice."*
- **Ecclesiastes 4:9–12** – *"Two are better than one... a cord of three strands is not quickly broken."*
- **Hebrews 10:24–25** – *"Let us consider how to spur one another on..."*

These cards help you foster *a culture of care*. They remind your team to stay connected, stay honest, and stay mutually invested.

When relationships thrive, success follows.

Diamonds: Wealth Building (13 cards)

Because financial overflow is a Kingdom responsibility, not just a personal goal.

Diamonds represent *God's provision, wisdom, and strategy for creating wealth*. These verses remind us that generating income isn't unspiritual—it's stewardship. Wealth isn't about excess. It's about equipping others and funding the mission.

Key Scriptures include:

- **Deuteronomy 8:18** – *"He gives you the power to get wealth."*
- **Proverbs 13:22** – *"A good man leaves an inheritance to his children's children."*
- **Matthew 25:14–30** – *The Parable of the Talents—multiply what you've been given.*
- **Malachi 3:10–11** – *"Bring the whole tithe… I will open the windows of heaven."*

These cards encourage responsible growth, wise investment, and faith-based financial planning. They keep wealth-building rooted in *purpose*, not pressure.

And they empower your team to build businesses that *bless others.*

Clubs: Leadership (13 cards)

Because every movement needs structure—and every team needs someone to say, "Let's go."

Clubs focus on the role of leadership—servant leadership, bold leadership, ethical leadership. These verses encourage courage, accountability, and the kind of inner strength that helps teams *rise together.*

Key Scriptures include:

- **Nehemiah 2:17–18** – *"Let us rise and build."*
- **Proverbs 27:17** – *"As iron sharpens iron, so one person sharpens another."*
- **1 Timothy 3:1–7** – *"Here is a trustworthy saying: If anyone sets his heart on being an overseer..."*
- **Joshua 1:9** – *"Be strong and courageous."*

Leadership isn't reserved for titles. Every team member can lead by example. These cards help stir up the leadership qualities in everyone—and help you raise up others, too.

Strong leaders create strong teams.

And strong teams change lives.

Spades: Success (13 cards)

Because fruit matters—and God wants His people to flourish.

Finally, the suit of **Spades** centers on *biblical success*. These verses reframe success—not as worldly achievement, but as alignment with God's promises. They remind your team that God *wants* to bless the work of your hands—and that success can be both holy and sustainable.

Key Scriptures include:

- **Jeremiah 29:11** – *"Plans to prosper you, not to harm you."*
- **Romans 8:28** – *"All things work together for good."*
- **Philippians 4:19** – *"God will supply all your needs..."*
- **3 John 1:2** – *"That you may prosper and be in good health, just as your soul prospers."*

These cards ignite hope. They reset mindsets. They cast vision for what's possible when you build with God, not just for God.

And they help your team keep dreaming—even when challenges arise.

The Card Format: Simplicity with Purpose

Every card follows the same accessible structure:

- **Title** – a one-line focus (like "Build Together" or "Overflow Mindset")
- **Application:** a short phrase that offers how to use or reflect on the verse
- **Scripture:** the core verse—clear, bold, powerful

This format makes it easy to share, teach, discuss, and apply—whether in a team meeting, morning devotional, or small group.

It's not overwhelming. It's actionable.

Because the goal isn't to impress—it's to *equip.*

This Isn't Just a Deck—It's a Strategy

The *Mutual Success Scriptures* deck isn't a random collection. It's a Kingdom-aligned curriculum.

It trains your team.

It nurtures your culture.

It brings clarity, direction, encouragement, and unity.

And most of all—it puts the Word of God at the center of everything you build.

This is your foundational deck.

Use it often. Teach from it. Pass it around. Let it shape your team's language and lifestyle.

Because when the Word becomes your strategy—*success becomes inevitable.*

Part 4: The Deck – Cards Showcase

Here's where the vision becomes tangible. In this section, you'll see every card in the new "Mutual Success Team" deck—laid out with scripture, application, and purpose.

Each card is a tool. Not just for games, but for devotionals, conversation starters, small groups, family bonding, and training your team in spiritual and practical truths. These cards were carefully designed to align with the four suits—each one reinforcing a key pillar of Mutual Success.

You'll see verses that build faith, inspire action, and help your team become stronger, wealthier, more unified, and more successful—in God's way. These aren't random selections. They're strategic scriptures, chosen for impact and transformation.

As you read through the showcase, think about how you'll use these cards. Will they be part of your morning routine? A gift to others? A tool in your group meetings? However you use them, this deck is designed to build both spiritual momentum and business success.

Chapter 24 – The Card Showcase: Showing All 54 Cards

A full walk-through of the deck that helps build faith, teams, and lasting success.

You've seen the heart behind the deck—now it's time to see the cards themselves. This chapter is your front-row seat to every verse, every application, every theme inside the *Mutual Success Scriptures* deck.

Each card is designed to speak directly into your life and team. With scripture on one side and a simple application on the other, these cards are both powerful and practical. Use them for devotionals, training, encouragement, or daily reminders. This is the Word—*in your hands, in your rhythm, and on mission with you.*

The "Mutual Success Team" Deck

2 ♠ Let All Things Work for Good

Application: Even setbacks become setups—when you love God, nothing is wasted in your journey.

Scripture: Romans 8:28 (NIV): "And we know that in all things God works for the good of those who love Him..."

2 ♠ Let All Things Work for Good

The "Mutual Success Team" Deck

3 ♠ Expect God to Meet Your Needs

Application: Trust His provision—Your Source is not your job—it's your Heavenly Father.

Scripture: Philippians 4:19: "And my God will meet all your needs according to the riches of His glory in Christ Jesus."

3 ♠ Expect God to Meet Your Needs

The "Mutual Success Team" Deck

4 ♠ Prosper in Soul, Body, and Purpose

Application: True success touches every area of your life—inside and out.

Scripture: 3 John 1:2 (NIV): "I pray that you may enjoy good health and that all may go well with you..."

4 ♠ Prosper in Soul, Body, and Purpose

The "Mutual Success Team" Deck

5 ♠ Remain Faithful With Little

Application: Every great breakthrough begins with small faithfulness—Steward well, and God multiplies.

Scripture: Luke 16:10 (NIV): "Whoever can be trusted with very little can also be trusted with much..."

5 ♠ Remain Faithful With Little

The "Mutual Success Team" Deck

6 ♠ Take Delight in the Lord

Application: When God is your joy, success becomes sweeter, simpler, and fully aligned with Heaven.

Scripture: Psalm 37:4 (NIV): "Take delight in the Lord, and He will give you the desires of your heart."

6 Take Delight in the Lord

The "Mutual Success Team" Deck

7 ♠ Ask Boldly, Believe Completely

Application: Your success is fueled by faith—God honors those who believe Him for big things.

Scripture: Mark 11:24 (NIV): "Whatever you ask for in prayer, believe that you have received it, and it will be yours."

7 Ask Boldly, Believe Completely

The "Mutual Success Team" Deck

8 ♠ Be Strong and Finish Well

Application: Stay faithful to your mission—don't quit halfway—God strengthens those who endure.

Scripture: 2 Chronicles 15:7: "But as for you, be strong and do not give up, for your work will be rewarded."

8 Be Strong and Finish Well

The "Mutual Success Team" Deck

9 ♠ Keep Your Hands Diligent

Application: Lazy hands miss opportunity—diligence unlocks increase and long-term fruit.

Scripture: Proverbs 10:4 (NIV): "Lazy hands make for poverty, but diligent hands bring wealth."

9 Keep Your Hands Diligent

The "Mutual Success Team" Deck

10 ♠ Speak Life Over Your Work

Application: Your words shape your world—declare what God says, not what fear says.

Scripture: Proverbs 18:21 (NIV): "The tongue has the power of life and death, and those who love it will eat its fruit."

10 Speak Life Over Your Work

The "Mutual Success Team" Deck

J ♠ Run the Race With Purpose

Application: Don't compare. Run your assignment, your lane, your mission. That's where your success lives.

Scripture: 1 Corinthians 9:24: "Run in such a way as to get the prize."

J Run the Race With Purpose

The "Mutual Success Team" Deck

Q ♠ Stay Rooted and Bear Fruit

Application: Success flows from staying connected to God—fruitfulness follows deep roots, not hustle.

Scripture: John 15:5 (NIV): "If you remain in Me and I in you, you will bear much fruit..."

Q Stay Rooted and Bear Fruit

The "Mutual Success Team" Deck

K ♠ Walk in Wisdom and Favor

Application: Wise actions lead to lasting success—Seek God's wisdom before you seek progress.

Scripture: Proverbs 3:5–6 (NIV): "Trust in the Lord with all your heart...and He will make your paths straight."

K Walk in Wisdom and Favor

The "Mutual Success Team" Deck

2 ♥ Lift Each Other Through Every Struggle

Application: When one member is discouraged or suffering, the whole team carries that weight—together.

Scripture: 1 Corinthians 12:26: "If one part suffers, every part suffers with it; if one part is honored, every part rejoices with it."

2 ♥ Lift Each Other Through Every Struggle

The "Mutual Success Team" Deck

3 ♥ Build Together—Don't Walk Alone

Application: Mutual Success means partnering in the work. Together, you're stronger, safer, and more effective.

Scripture: Ecclesiastes 4:9: "Two are better than one, because they have a good return for their labor..."

3 ♥ Build Together—Don't Walk Alone

The "Mutual Success Team" Deck

4 ♥ Spur Each Other Toward Growth

Application: A strong team doesn't just support—they challenge, sharpen, and push each other to rise.

Scripture: Hebrews 10:24 (NIV): "And let us consider how we may spur one another on toward love and good deeds..."

4 ♥ Spur Each Other Toward Growth

The "Mutual Success Team" Deck

5 ♥ Carry the Mission with One Voice

Application: Community power multiplies when everyone commits to the same mission with full-hearted agreement.

Scripture: Romans 15:6 (NIV): "So that with one mind and one voice you may glorify the God and Father of our Lord Jesus Christ."

5 ♥ Carry the Mission with One Voice

The "Mutual Success Team" Deck

6 ♥ Encourage One Another Daily

Application: Regular encouragement keeps momentum strong and prevents spiritual drift within the team.

Scripture: Hebrews 3:13 (NIV): "But encourage one another daily...so that none of you may be hardened by sin's deceitfulness."

6 Encourage One Another Daily

The "Mutual Success Team" Deck

7 ♥ Share What You Have Freely

Application: God provides more than enough when we each bring our time, resources, and love to the table.

Scripture: Acts 2:44–45 (NIV): "They sold property and possessions to give to anyone who had need."

7 Share What You Have Freely

The "Mutual Success Team" Deck

8 ♥ Pray Over Each Other's Work

Application: In a Mutual Success Team, we intercede for each other's projects like they're our own.

Scripture: James 5:16 (NIV): "Pray for each other so that you may be healed—The prayer of a righteous person is powerful..."

8 Pray Over Each Other's Work

The "Mutual Success Team" Deck

9 ♥ Speak Life Into Each Other

Application: Community means reminding each other of your identity, your calling, and God's promises.

Scripture: Proverbs 18:21 (NIV): "The tongue has the power of life and death, and those who love it will eat its fruit."

9 Speak Life Into Each Other

The "Mutual Success Team" Deck

10 ♥ Rejoice in Each Other's Victories

Application: When one team member wins, the whole team celebrates—success is shared, not siloed.

Scripture: Romans 12:15 (NIV): "Rejoice with those who rejoice; mourn with those who mourn."

10 ♥ Rejoice in Each Other's Victories

The "Mutual Success Team" Deck

J ♥ Stay Accountable Without Shame

Application: True love includes honesty—We grow stronger by holding each other to truth—with grace.

Scripture: Proverbs 27:6 (NIV): "Wounds from a friend can be trusted, but an enemy multiplies kisses."

J ♥ Stay Accountable Without Shame

The "Mutual Success Team" Deck

Q ♥ Make Room for Every Gift

Application: In a Kingdom team, everyone brings something that matters—no role is too small.

Scripture: 1 Peter 4:10 (NIV): "Each of you should use whatever gift you have received to serve others..."

Q ♥ Make Room for Every Gift

The "Mutual Success Team" Deck

K ♥ Be the Kind of Team God Blesses

Application: When we live like the early church—unified, generous, and full of faith—God adds increase.

Scripture: Acts 2:47 (NIV): "And the Lord added to their number daily those who were being saved."

K ♥ Be the Kind of Team God Blesses

The "Mutual Success Team" Deck

A ♠ Embrace God's Plan for Your Future

Application: Success begins with trust—God's plans are filled with purpose, peace, and divine hope.

Scripture: Jeremiah 29:11 (NIV): "For I know the plans I have for you...plans to prosper you...to give you hope and a future."

A ♠ Embrace God's Plan for Your Future

The "Mutual Success Team" Deck

A ♥ Be One in Heart and Purpose

Application: The foundation of a Mutual Success Team is unity—shared purpose, shared prayer, shared reward.

Scripture: Acts 4:32 (NIV): "All the believers were one in heart and mind..."

A ♥ Be One in Heart and Purpose

The "Mutual Success Team" Deck

JOKER

About The **"Mutual Success Team"** Cards

A powerful, purpose-filled deck created to build strong teams through faith—unlocking God's blessings together.

JOKER

About The "Mutual Success Team" Cards

The "Mutual Success Team" Deck

JOKER

Christian™ Decks

The "Mutual Success" Series is a Bible scripture based collection - to help us all mutually succeed.

www.ChristianDecks.com

Published by Christianity Publications

JOKER

Christian™ Decks

The "Mutual Success Team" Deck

2 ♣ Sharpen One Another Consistently

Application: Accountability and growth happen when leaders challenge and refine each other in love.

Scripture: Proverbs 27:17 (NIV): "As iron sharpens iron, so one person sharpens another."

2 ♣ Sharpen One Another Consistently

The "Mutual Success Team" Deck

3 ♣ Live What You Lead

Application: Leadership starts with example—Let your life match your words, goals, and faith.

Scripture: 1 Timothy 4:12 (NIV): "Set an example for the believers in speech, in conduct, in love, in faith and in purity."

3 ♣ Live What You Lead

The "Mutual Success Team" Deck

4 ♣ Be Courageous When It Counts

Application: A leader stands strong when others hesitate—Trust God's strength to carry you forward.

Scripture: Joshua 1:9 (NIV): "Be strong and courageous... For the Lord your God will be with you wherever you go."

4 ♣ Be Courageous When It Counts

The "Mutual Success Team" Deck

5 ♣ Serve Before You Lead

Application: In the Kingdom, leadership begins with service—humble action always outranks titles.

Scripture: Mark 10:45 (NIV): "For even the Son of Man did not come to be served, but to serve..."

5 ♣ Serve Before You Lead

The "Mutual Success Team" Deck

6 ♣ **Build Up, Don't Tear Down**

Application: Leaders use their voice to encourage, correct with grace, and strengthen the whole team.

Scripture: Ephesians 4:29 (NIV): "Do not let any unwholesome talk come out of your mouths, but only what is helpful..."

6 ♣ Build Up, Don't Tear Down

The "Mutual Success Team" Deck

7 ♣ **Stay Above Reproach**

Application: Live with integrity, honesty, and discipline—this earns trust and protects your influence.

Scripture: 1 Timothy 3:2 (NIV): "Now the overseer is to be above reproach, faithful to his wife, temperate, self-controlled..."

7 ♣ Stay Above Reproach

The "Mutual Success Team" Deck

8 ♣ **Speak Boldly for What's Right**

Application: Don't be silent when truth is on the line—courageous leadership requires clear conviction.

Scripture: Acts 4:29 (NIV): "Enable Your servants to speak Your word with great boldness."

8 ♣ Speak Boldly for What's Right

The "Mutual Success Team" Deck

9 ♣ **Be Led by the Holy Spirit**

Application: Human plans fail—Spirit-led leaders listen, obey, and adjust to God's direction quickly.

Scripture: Galatians 5:25 (NIV): "Since we live by the Spirit, let us keep in step with the Spirit."

9 ♣ Be Led by the Holy Spirit

The "Mutual Success Team" Deck

10 ♣ Own the Responsibility, Share the Credit

Application: Leaders step up in tough times, and lift others up when success comes.

Scripture: Philippians 2:3 (NIV): "In humility value others above yourselves..."

10 Own the Responsibility, Share the Credit

The "Mutual Success Team" Deck

J ♣ Prepare the Next Leader Now

Application: Great leaders think generationally—train others to lead even better than you.

Scripture: 2 Timothy 2:2 (NIV): "...Entrust to reliable people who will also be qualified to teach others."

J Prepare the Next Leader Now

The "Mutual Success Team" Deck

Q ♣ Manage God's People with Care

Application: Leaders aren't owners—they're stewards—Treat people with respect, value, and spiritual responsibility.

Scripture: 1 Peter 5:2 (NIV): "Be shepherds of God's flock...not lording it over those entrusted to you..."

Q Manage God's People with Care

The "Mutual Success Team" Deck

K ♣ Walk in Authority With Humility

Application: Lead boldly, but stay submitted to God—real power flows from reverence, not pride.

Scripture: James 4:10 (NIV): "Humble yourselves before the Lord, and He will lift you up."

K Walk in Authority With Humility

The "Mutual Success Team" Deck

2 ♦ Leave a Legacy That Lasts

Application: Think beyond your lifetime—Wealth should bless future generations and advance God's mission.

Scripture: Proverbs 13:22 (NIV): "A good person leaves an inheritance for their children's children..."

2 ♦ Leave a Legacy That Lasts

The "Mutual Success Team" Deck

3 ♦ Multiply What God Gave You

Application: Don't bury your gifts—use, grow, and invest them for God's glory and team success.

Scripture: Matthew 25:21 (NIV): "Well done...You have been faithful with a few things; I will put you in charge of many things..."

3 ♦ Multiply What God Gave You

The "Mutual Success Team" Deck

4 ♦ Use Money to Lift Others Up

Application: Giving isn't a rule—it's a joy. When you're able, use your money to bless someone's day.

Scripture: 1 Timothy 6:18 (NIV): "Command them to do good, to be rich in good deeds, and to be generous and willing to share."

4 ♦ Use Money to Lift Others Up

The "Mutual Success Team" Deck

5 ♦ Work With Diligence and Purpose

Application: Wealth comes through consistent, purposeful work—done in faith and with excellence.

Scripture: Proverbs 10:4 (NIV): "Lazy hands make for poverty, but diligent hands bring wealth."

5 ♦ Work With Diligence and Purpose

The "Mutual Success Team" Deck

6 ♦ Use Money to Bless Others

Application: Money is a tool—Use it to help your team, support the poor, and spread the Gospel.

Scripture: Proverbs 11:25 (NIV): "A generous person will prosper; whoever refreshes others will be refreshed."

6 ♦ Use Money to Bless Others

The "Mutual Success Team" Deck

7 ♦ Seek Wisdom Before Wealth

Application: Don't chase riches—seek wisdom—God's ways lead to lasting and righteous increase.

Scripture: Proverbs 3:13–14: "Blessed are those who find wisdom...She is more profitable than silver..."

7 ♦ Seek Wisdom Before Wealth

The "Mutual Success Team" Deck

8 ♦ Track What You Steward

Application: Know your numbers—Responsible teams track income, costs, and goals to grow together.

Scripture: Proverbs 27:23 (NIV): "Be sure you know the condition of your flocks, give careful attention to your herds..."

8 ♦ Track What You Steward

The "Mutual Success Team" Deck

9 ♦ Avoid Debt That Weighs You Down

Application: Debt is a trap—Build slowly with peace, not pressure—freedom is better than fast.

Scripture: Proverbs 22:7 (NIV): "The borrower is slave to the lender."

9 ♦ Avoid Debt That Weighs You Down

The "Mutual Success Team" Deck

10 ♦ Don't Serve Money—Master It

Application: Your team should manage money well, but never let it rule decisions or direction.

Scripture: Matthew 6:24 (NIV): "You cannot serve both God and money."

10 ♦ Don't Serve Money—Master It

The "Mutual Success Team" Deck

J ♦ Give First—Then Grow More

Application: Kingdom wealth multiplies when you give from the start—not just when you feel ready.

Scripture: Luke 6:38 (NIV): "Give, and it will be given to you...For with the measure you use, it will be measured to you."

J ♦ Give First—Then Grow More

The "Mutual Success Team" Deck

Q ♦ Build for Others, Not Just Yourself

Application: True wealth builds people, not just profits—Invest in lives, not only in returns.

Scripture: Philippians 2:4 (NIV): "Not looking to your own interests but each of you to the interests of the others."

Q ♦ Build for Others, Not Just Yourself

The "Mutual Success Team" Deck

K ♦ Let God Lead Your Finances

Application: Your budget, plans, and decisions belong to God—submit them to Him and watch peace grow.

Scripture: Proverbs 16:3 (NIV): "Commit to the Lord whatever you do, and He will establish your plans."

K ♦ Let God Lead Your Finances

The "Mutual Success Team" Deck

A ♦ Trust God as Your Source

Application: Wealth begins with trusting God—not hustle—He empowers your team to build and prosper.

Scripture: Deuteronomy 8:18: "...For it is He Who gives you the ability to produce wealth..."

A ♦ Trust God as Your Source

The "Mutual Success Team" Deck

A ♣ Lead the Charge With Vision

Application: Great leaders don't wait—they act with clarity, invite others in, and cast Kingdom-focused vision.

Scripture: Nehemiah 2:17–18: "Let us start rebuilding...So they began this good work."

A ♣ Lead the Charge With Vision

Part 5: The Tools – What You Need To Succeed

Every great mission needs the right tools. This part equips you with everything practical—so your project moves from idea to income without confusion or delay.

You'll start by choosing your method—based on your skills, personality, and time. We'll help you map out your first steps, avoid common mistakes, and even provide scripts to make your first conversations easy and natural.

Then we'll show you how to scale—how to turn one small success into repeat customers, passive income, and a team that sells alongside you. These tools help you move faster and smarter, while building a business that's sustainable.

If you've ever felt like you needed a mentor to walk you through a plan, this section is it. Follow it step-by-step, and you'll find yourself building momentum you can't wait to share.

Chapter 25 – Choosing Your Method – Part 1: Finding the Fit That Matches Your Life

You don't need to become someone else to succeed. You just need to find your lane—and run with it.

"Where do I start?"

That's the most common question people ask when they're first introduced to Christian Decks as a Mutual Success Project. And it's a fair question.

With over 100+ possible ways to sell and share Scripture Decks (which we'll explore in depth in Part 7), the hardest part isn't lack of opportunity—it's choosing *where to begin.*

This chapter is here to help you do exactly that.

Because you don't have to guess your way into success. You don't have to copy what someone else did. You don't have to waste time trying method after method hoping something sticks.

Instead, we're going to show you how to discover the strategy that fits *you.*

Not just your availability. Not just your skill set.

But your *personality*. Your lifestyle. Your comfort zone. Your strengths.

Because success isn't found by becoming someone else.

It's found by becoming fully yourself—on purpose.

The Key Principle: There Is No One Right Way

Before we walk you through how to choose your method, let's set the record straight:

There is no "best" or "most effective" strategy.

What works for a stay-at-home mom may not work for a college student. What works for a pastor may not work for a quiet introvert. What works offline may not translate online—and vice versa.

And that's not a weakness of the system. That's the *strength* of it.

You're not trapped in a cookie-cutter business. You're being handed a customizable tool.

The real question is not, *"What's the most successful way to do this?"*
The better question is, *"What's the most natural way for me to start?"*

We'll help you answer that.

Because once you find the method that fits your life, everything gets easier.

Conversations flow.

Momentum builds.

And most importantly—*you enjoy it.*

Use This Simple Decision Tree to Find Your Fit

Let's walk through a few simple questions. Each answer will guide you toward a method category that's already proven and ready for you to personalize.

1. Do you prefer talking to people face-to-face, or working behind the scenes?

- *Face-to-face?* → Look at **in-person methods** (booths, one-on-one sharing, local events, church partnerships).
- *Behind the scenes?* → Try **online or creative approaches** (social media, email sharing, content creation).

2. Are you more consistent in digital spaces or physical ones?

- *Digital?* → Consider **affiliate links, YouTube, or Instagram reels**.
- *Physical?* → Try **gifting, small group meetups, or Scripture Deck tables at events.**

3. Do you prefer structure or spontaneity?

- *Structure?* → Choose a method you can schedule weekly—like a standing table after service or weekly email.
- *Spontaneity?* → Go with relationship-driven outreach—share as it comes up naturally in conversation.

4. Do you already have a community or platform?

- *Yes?* → Use that as your base. Don't overthink. Start there.
- *Not yet?* → Start small with gifting, direct messages, or finding 2–3 people to test a method with.

5. How much time can you invest right now?

- *5–10 minutes/day?* → Try posting 1 verse a day or gifting a deck each week.
- *1–2 hours/week?* → Set up a weekly email, short videos, or a physical spot to share decks.
- *More time?* → You might combine 2–3 approaches for faster scale (see next section).

This tree isn't meant to box you in—it's meant to reveal where *you already thrive.*

That's where you begin.

Combining Methods for Momentum

Some of the most effective Mutual Success Team builders don't use just one method—they **combine two or three**, using one as their "base," and the others to layer growth.

Here's how that might look:

- **Base method: In-person sharing at church**

- Layer 1: Post online once a week with a photo of the deck
- Layer 2: Keep a few decks in your bag for when conversations naturally arise

- **Base method: Affiliate link shared on social media**

- Layer 1: Add a personal video sharing how the deck helped you
- Layer 2: Invite your best customers to join your team and earn, too

- **Base method: Weekly small group devotion using the cards**

- Layer 1: Ask each member to share their favorite card during the week
- Layer 2: Create a one-pager with your method to share with other leaders

Combining methods does **not** mean doubling your effort.

It means **amplifying your impact** with small touches of consistency.

And the more natural those layers feel, the more you'll keep going.

How to Know You've Chosen the Right Method

When your method is aligned with your life, you'll know. It won't feel like friction. It will feel like flow.

You'll know you've found your fit when:

- You're consistent without forcing it
- You actually enjoy the way you share
- People respond naturally (not out of pressure)
- You can explain your method in one sentence

Here are a few real-life one-liners from people who found their fit:

- *"I use the deck in my youth group, and others always want to take one home."*
- *"I just post one verse a day on Facebook—people message me asking where I got it."*
- *"I offer a deck to every customer who visits my small business."*

When it's that simple, you'll *stick with it.*

And when you stick with it, *success follows.*

This Chapter Isn't Just Theory—It's a Starting Point

If you've been waiting to feel "ready," this is your permission to stop waiting.

You don't need to do everything.

You just need to do something that *fits who you already are.*

Pick your base method.

Add one layer if you're able.

Give yourself permission to learn, test, and grow as you go.

Because your perfect strategy isn't out there waiting to be found.

It's already inside you—waiting to be released.

Let's discover it together.

Chapter 26 – Choosing Your Method – Part 2: Test, Refine, and Set a Real Plan

The right method isn't just chosen—it's proven, step-by-step. This is how you find your traction and keep moving forward.

You've chosen your starting point. Now it's time to find your rhythm.

If the last chapter helped you discover which method fits your life, this one helps you *build momentum with it.*

Because choosing the right method is only the first step. Next, you have to bring it into the real world—*test it*, see how it lands, and refine it until it flows.

This chapter isn't about hustling harder or launching with pressure. It's about building *confidently* by learning what works for you through **small experiments, light tracking, and simple adjustments**.

It's about getting real results without burnout, and setting a clear plan you can actually follow.

Because consistency isn't born out of perfection—it's born out of *clarity and progress.*

Let's start building your plan—step by step.

Step 1: Set a "Test Window" to Try Your Method

Here's the first move: decide on a short time window to test your method.

We recommend starting with **7 days to 30 days**, depending on your availability and comfort level. This "test window" isn't about performance—it's about *exploration*.

Ask yourself:

- What method am I trying first?
- How many times per week will I use it?
- What counts as a win? (i.e., someone responding, asking a question, making a purchase, or sharing a deck)

Example Test Window Plan:

- *Method:* Posting Scripture Deck reflections on Instagram
- *Window:* 14 days
- *Plan:* 1 post every 2 days
- *Success signal:* 3 comments, 2 direct messages, or 1 order

You're not guessing. You're not going forever. You're testing—intentionally.

This makes the process feel safe. Measurable. Clear.

And that clarity removes overwhelm.

Step 2: Track What Works (and What Doesn't)

During your test window, use a simple journal or digital note to track your activity. Don't overcomplicate it.

Here's what to record:

- What did I do today?
- How long did it take?
- What was the result?
- How did I feel doing it?

That last question is *critical.*

Some methods work, but feel exhausting. Others may be slower at first—but feel *natural and energizing.* That's a sign you've found something sustainable.

What to look for:

- Conversations that flowed easily
- Comments or responses from others
- Repeat questions or curiosity

- Decks shared or sold
- Unexpected doors that opened

The data doesn't lie. And when you look at it with faith and honesty, you'll start to see patterns.

You'll know what to repeat—and what to tweak.

That's where traction is born.

Step 3: Refine—One Layer at a Time

After your test window, it's time to refine.

Start by asking:

- What felt easy?
- What got a response?
- What took too much energy?
- What could I adjust next time?

Then make one change at a time. Add a layer. Remove friction. Clarify your message.

Examples of simple refinements:

- Change when you post or message (morning vs. evening)
- Add a question or reflection to your message
- Try a different opening line or follow-up approach
- Shorten your explanation of the deck

- Offer a bonus (free card, digital printable, or prayer note)

Refinement isn't reinvention. It's **small, smart upgrades** to the method that already fits your life.

The goal is not to chase someone else's results.

The goal is to **optimize your rhythm**—until it starts to feel automatic.

Step 4: Set Small, Encouraging Goals You Can Actually Hit

Here's where most people trip: they set goals that sound impressive... but feel discouraging two weeks later.

Let's fix that.

You don't need a big vision right now. You need *a doable goal that builds belief.*

Here are some examples of *great first goals:*

- Share your method with 3 friends
- Sell or gift 5 decks this month
- Try your method 3 times in 1 week
- Have one person say, "This helped me"
- Post one scripture with your story attached

Small wins compound. They build momentum. And they keep you in motion.

That's why your goals need to be *visible* and *celebrated*.

Write them down. Keep them on your fridge. Share them with your Mutual Success Team. Mark them off as they happen.

Let it be fun.

Let it build your faith.

Step 5: Choose a Simple Tracking Habit

Here's a game-changer: track your progress weekly—not obsessively.

At the end of each week, ask yourself:

- What did I try?
- What worked?
- What didn't?
- What's one thing I'll repeat next week?

That's it.

Five minutes of reflection gives you a full week of direction.

You'll stay grounded. You'll stay encouraged. And you'll stop drifting into guesswork.

This is how successful people keep winning—they *measure with kindness and clarity*.

You don't need fancy spreadsheets.

You just need one page and a pen.

Or a note in your phone.

This one habit turns ideas into *progress.*

Success Isn't a Secret. It's a Sequence.

Test.
Track.
Refine.
Repeat.

That's it.

You don't need to be loud. You don't need to be pushy. You don't need to reinvent the wheel.

You just need to try one thing, learn from it, and adjust.

Over and over.

Before long, you'll have a method that works, a rhythm that flows, and a track record that tells you—*you're doing it right.*

This is how confidence grows.

This is how consistency forms.

This is how your Mutual Success Project becomes real.

One test at a time.

Chapter 27 – Getting Started Fast – Part 1: Your First Week and What You Actually Need

No more guessing. No more overthinking. This is your 7-day plan to launch with clarity, confidence, and traction.

"I'm ready to start... but what do I actually do first?"

That question hits hard. You're excited. You believe in the mission. You see the potential. But when it's time to begin, your brain says: *"Wait... what do I actually need to do today?"*

That's what this chapter is here to solve.

You don't need to guess. You don't need to second-guess. And you don't need to over-plan.

You just need a simple, clear roadmap for your first week—a set of steps you can follow without pressure or perfection.

We'll also give you a short list of what you *actually need* to get started—so you're not spinning your wheels gathering supplies or trying to make it fancy before it's functional.

This is your seven-day launch plan. And by the end of it, you'll have traction, confidence, and a sense of rhythm that tells you: *"Yes. I can really do this."*

Let's begin.

Day 1 – Get Your Deck, Get Your Vision

Start by putting the Word in your hand.

✔ Order or print your first Scripture Deck
✔ Take 10 minutes to flip through it—ask God which card speaks to your life right now
✔ Write down your "why"—why you're doing this, who you want to help, and what success would feel like for you

What this day is about: alignment. This isn't just business—it's *purpose*. Take a moment to reconnect to your heart. You're not just moving product. You're moving *people* closer to the Word.

Optional: Take a photo of the card that stood out to you. This might become your first post later.

Day 2 – Choose Your Method and Set Up Your Space

✔ Re-read Chapter 25 and 26 if needed
✔ Choose one primary method to begin with (digital post, conversation starter, gift outreach, church table, etc.)
✔ Set up your "Scripture Deck Zone"—a bag, drawer, or section of your desk where you'll keep your cards and materials

What this day is about: simplicity. Don't try five things at once. Choose one thing that fits your life. Create a spot where your materials live. Clear space = clear mind.

Day 3 – Share a Card with One Person

✔ Pick one person who could use encouragement
✔ Text them a photo of the card or hand it to them in person
✔ Say something real and kind: "This verse helped me today—thought of you."

What this day is about: connection. You're not selling yet. You're sowing. You're building trust. You're seeing how it feels to share without pressure.

Optional: Ask how it spoke to them. Listen. Let the response guide your next move.

Day 4 – Make Your First Post (or Verbal Share)

✔ If you're sharing online, post a photo or story about your favorite card
✔ Keep it real—no pressure, no hype
✔ If you're sharing offline, tell someone face-to-face how these cards encouraged you

What this day is about: visibility. People can't respond to what they don't know exists. Whether online or in-person, take one step toward letting the world know what you're doing—and why.

You don't need to "sell." You just need to *show up.*

Day 5 – Prepare for Sales (Just in Case)

✔ Order or prep 5 extra decks (or know how to quickly order more if interest picks up)
✔ Create a simple note or flyer that explains the deck and includes a way to order
✔ Have a pen and notebook ready to track names or messages from interested people

What this day is about: readiness. You may not get a sale today—but when it comes, you want to be prepared. That *confidence* will show in your conversations.

Optional: Write out a one-line explanation:

"These are 52 powerful scriptures for encouragement and connection—one for each week or moment."

Day 6 – Reach Out to 3 More People

✔ Think of 3 people who love scripture, lead others, or need a lift
✔ Send a short message with a photo or question:

"Have you ever seen these? I've started using them and thought of you."

✔ Don't pitch. Just invite.

What this day is about: rhythm. Now you're repeating what works. You're gently expanding. You're finding who responds. And you're getting more comfortable every time.

Day 7 – Reflect and Reset

✔ Write down what you did this week
✔ List what felt easy, what worked, what surprised you
✔ Choose your next 3-day mini goal (Example: "Share with 5 people this week," or "Make 1 sale and follow up")

What this day is about: celebration. You did it. You *started*. And even if it didn't feel big, it was *faithful*. Now it's time to build from here.

What You Actually Need to Start

Let's keep your supply list light and focused. Here's what's *actually useful*:

✓ **At least 1 physical Scripture Deck** – for you to use and show others
✓ **Pen and small notebook** – to track who you've shared with, ideas, and wins
✓ **Phone or device with a camera** – to take and share card photos
✓ **Small bag or box** – to carry decks or handouts with you
✓ **Order link or form** – either digital or printed, so people know how to get their own
✓ **Basic handout or info sheet** (optional) – short explanation + contact info + ordering instructions
✓ **Bonus:** An encouraging mindset and a reason for starting ☺

You don't need fancy. You don't need to "launch."

You just need to begin—and this list is more than enough.

The First Week Is Where Confidence Begins

You don't need a big team yet. You don't need momentum yet.

You just need motion.

This plan gives you exactly that.

You're not doing this randomly—you're walking through a proven, simple first step that puts you in position for something real to grow.

So give yourself permission to be new. Let the awkward moments be okay. Let the small wins count as big victories.

Because the truth is: you've already started.

And now, you're just building forward.

Chapter 28 – Getting Started Fast – Part 2: What to Say, What to Avoid, and How to Stay Natural

You don't have to be a talker. You just have to be honest—and that's what makes it work.

"But what do I actually say?"

That's one of the most common fears when people first start sharing Scripture Decks. They believe in the mission. They love the product. But they freeze when it's time to talk about it.

They worry about sounding awkward.

They worry about "getting in the way."

They worry about turning a spiritual moment into a sales pitch.

So they stay silent. Not because they lack faith—but because they don't yet feel *confident in their words*.

This chapter is here to fix that.

Because you don't need to become someone else to share Scripture Decks.

You just need a few simple phrases—rooted in truth, not hype—that open doors, create ease, and let people experience the product for themselves.

You'll also learn the most common mistakes new sellers make (and how to avoid them), so you can move forward with *peace, clarity, and momentum.*

Let's get you talking—*your way.*

The Core Principle: Speak From Experience, Not Pressure

People can tell the difference between a pitch and a personal share.

A pitch feels like it has an agenda. A personal share feels like it has *heart.*

That's why we start every script and conversation here: **what has this done for you?**

Did it encourage you this week?

Did a certain card stand out?

Did someone else respond to it in a surprising way?

Let your experience guide your words. When you speak from your *story*, you won't sound like a salesperson. You'll sound like a friend.

And that's what opens doors.

Practice Scripts That Sound Like You

Use these as a starting point. Adapt them. Make them your own. Say them how you'd naturally talk.

1. One-on-One (friend, family, church member):

"Hey, I started using these Scripture Cards during my quiet time—just one verse a day. They've honestly helped me stay focused when I'm distracted. I thought of you because I know you love scripture too."

2. When gifting a deck:

"This is something I've been using—it's simple, but powerful. Each card has a verse and a short message. I thought you might enjoy flipping through it when you need a lift."

3. For online sharing (social media):

"This is the card I pulled today. I didn't expect it, but it was exactly what I needed. I've been using these decks to help me stay in the

Word when I'm busy. Let me know if you want one—I can send you the info."

4. For casual text message:

"Thought you might like this. I've been using these scripture cards for quick encouragement—super simple but surprisingly meaningful."

5. For a church announcement or small group share:

"We've started using these scripture decks as a way to stay in the Word daily. They're easy to use, and even easier to share. If you're looking for a way to build faith throughout the week, I've got some I'd love to show you."

Pro Tip: Don't end with "Would you like to buy one?"
End with **an open door**:

"Let me know if you want to check them out."
"You can flip through mine if you want to see how they work."
"If this feels like something helpful, I can show you where to get one."

Low pressure. High peace.

That's what people trust.

Conversation Starters That Open Spiritual Space

Sometimes the best way to lead into the deck isn't to *start with the deck*. It's to start with the *person*.

Try questions like:

- "What's a verse that's carried you lately?"
- "How do you stay grounded in the Word during busy seasons?"
- "Ever find it hard to keep a devotional rhythm going?"
- "What helps you feel encouraged when life feels a little chaotic?"

These are *real questions*—and they open real conversations.

Once the person shares, you can simply say:

"That's exactly why I started using these Scripture Cards. They keep it simple, but meaningful. Want to see one?"

This is *evangelism through empathy.*
Business through blessing.
And it works.

Common Mistakes to Avoid (So You Can Build Confidence Early)

Here are the traps that new sellers sometimes fall into—plus how to sidestep them gracefully:

1. Trying to sound "salesy."
Don't memorize product specs. Don't over-explain. Just share why it's helped you. Let them ask more if they're curious.

2. Talking too much.
Keep it brief. People don't need a lecture—they need a *moment*. One story. One verse. One offer to learn more.

3. Waiting for perfection.
Don't stall until you've crafted the perfect message. Progress comes through *action*, not polish.

4. Assuming people aren't interested.
You might be surprised who responds. Don't disqualify anyone. Plant the seed and let God water it.

5. Focusing only on the sale.
Every share is a *win*, even if they don't buy right away. Encourage. Inspire. Stay consistent. The fruit will follow.

6. Talking only about the product, not the person.
Remember: people don't care what you're offering until they know *you care about them*. Lead with love, not logistics.

Your Words Matter—But They Don't Have to Be Perfect

Here's the truth: people will forget your exact phrasing.

But they won't forget how you made them feel.

When you share Scripture Decks with honesty and heart, you're doing more than making an offer—you're extending *encouragement*. You're speaking life. You're planting truth.

Even if they say no today, they'll remember the *way you showed up*.

And when the time is right, they'll come back.

So be gentle with yourself. Be real with others.

And trust the process.

Let Your Voice Be a Vessel

God doesn't need you to sound impressive.

He just needs you to be *available.*

So go ahead—open your mouth, send the message, hand someone a card, post what blessed you.

You're not performing.

You're partnering—with truth, with the Spirit, and with a mission bigger than a single sale.

You don't need to say it "right."

You just need to say it *with love.*

Chapter 29 – Scaling Your Success – Part 1: Turning One-Time Sales into Repeat Customers

The first sale is just the beginning. The real growth comes when people come back—and bring others with them.

You made a few sales. Now what?

First of all—congratulations. Whether it was one deck or ten, something powerful just happened: you stepped into motion. You took what you believed in and put it in someone else's hands. That's no small thing.

But now, a new question arises:

How do I keep this going?

This chapter is your guide to answering that.

Because the key to sustainable income—and expanding impact—isn't just selling more. It's creating experiences that people want to come back to.

In other words: **repeat customers**.

The kind who don't just buy once, but again and again. The kind who share what you offer because they believe in it. The kind who say, "You've really helped me—what else do you have?"

When that happens, you move from *starter* to *scaler*.

Let's walk through how to make that shift with grace, joy, and clarity—while staying true to the mission.

Step 1: Make the First Experience Memorable

The biggest myth in business is that the sale ends when the money comes in.

But real success begins *after* the first purchase.

When someone receives your Scripture Deck, what happens next? Do they feel seen? Encouraged? Respected? Supported?

Here are simple ways to create a "wow" moment:

- **Include a handwritten note.** A simple "Thank you—may this bless your time with God" can mean everything.

- **Offer a tip sheet or card guide.** Help them know how to use it with ease.
- **Follow up with a short message.** A few days later, send a message: *"Just checking in—how are you liking the deck?"*

This may sound small—but these touches create emotional connection.

And when people feel that connection, they *remember you.*

They trust you.

And they come back.

Step 2: Create a Reason to Return

Once someone owns a Scripture Deck, what's next?

Your job is to *guide the journey forward*.

Here are a few ways to do that:

1. Offer complementary decks.
If they loved the first, let them know about new versions—like a deck for kids, for couples, or for team success.

2. Suggest a gift.
People often don't think about giving a deck until you say:

"Have you thought of gifting one to someone who needs encouragement?"

3. Offer group sets.
Let customers know they can use decks for Bible studies, team meetings, or small groups—and offer a small bulk discount to help.

4. Create themed bundles.
Pair decks with prayer journals, bookmarks, or printable cards. This increases perceived value and gives a reason to re-engage.

The goal is not to "sell more stuff."

It's to *meet more needs.*

And when people feel that—they don't just return... they *bring others with them.*

Step 3: Keep the Relationship Alive

Repeat customers come from *relationships*, not reminders.

So ask yourself: How can I stay connected with people I've already served?

Here are simple, non-intrusive ways:

- **Start an email list or text circle.** Let buyers opt in to receive weekly encouragement or scripture-based content.
- **Create a "Card of the Week" post.** Share a short reflection using the deck—customers will remember why they loved it in the first place.
- **Ask for feedback.** This not only improves your business, but makes people feel included in the journey.

You don't have to message everyone constantly.

You just have to *show up sometimes* with real value.

Because when they see you again and again, still grounded, still encouraging—they'll *trust you more*, and *buy again faster*.

Step 4: Build a Referral Mindset

The easiest way to grow your business is to **turn happy customers into helpers.**

If someone loves the deck, they'll naturally think of others who could use it. But you can make that process even easier.

Here's how:

- **Add a "give one, get one" offer.** If they refer a friend, you send them a thank-you or small bonus.

- **Create a referral card.** When you send their order, include an extra mini-card with a short message: *"Know someone who would love this? Here's a card to pass on."*
- **Follow up with gratitude.** When someone sends a friend your way, thank them personally. It builds goodwill—and loyalty.

Referrals are the fruit of **relational trust**.

And when you create a culture of encouragement, people will naturally want to *spread it.*

Step 5: Expand Methods Without Losing Focus

As your base grows, you may feel tempted to try a bunch of new methods.

That's not wrong—but it must be done *wisely.*

Here's the rule: **add methods gradually, not desperately.**

Once your primary method is flowing, consider:

- Turning social media posts into short reels
- Adding a table at a local event
- Creating a 1-page flyer to hand out at church
- Hosting a Scripture Deck devotional online
- Building a small team and training others to do what's working for you

But don't rush.

Expansion should feel like *an extension of what's working*—not a reaction to what's not.

Protect your energy.

Multiply what's fruitful.

And stay aligned with the rhythm that brought you success in the first place.

Repeat Customers Are Not a Mystery—They're a Mindset

Here's the secret most people overlook:

Repeat customers don't come from pressure.
They come from **presence**.
They come from consistency.
They come from a heart that truly wants to serve.

So if you've sold even one deck—celebrate that.

Now it's time to ask:

- How can I make this experience amazing?
- How can I stay in their world without being overwhelming?
- How can I meet a new need, or spark a new joy?

Do that, and you won't just build sales.

You'll build *community*.

And that's the kind of success that scales—and *lasts*.

Chapter 30 – Scaling Your Success – Part 2: Building Teams and Creating Long-Term Income

When you help others succeed, you multiply what's possible—and create income that lasts without chasing every sale yourself.

You've tasted success. Now you're ready to multiply it.

There comes a point in every journey where a shift happens—when it's no longer about what *you* can do alone, but what you can build *with others.*

That's the moment when your Scripture Deck efforts evolve from side project to system. From hustle to harmony. From temporary income... to something **permanent.**

That's what this chapter is all about.

Because the fastest, most sustainable way to scale is **not doing more yourself**—it's **building others up** to do what's already working.

When you start building a team—a *Mutual Success Team*—you unlock an entirely new level of growth. It's no longer just about one person selling. It's about *many people succeeding together*.

And when that happens?
Income becomes **passive**.
Impact becomes **exponential**.
And success becomes **shared**—the way it was always meant to be.

Let's explore exactly how to do that—without overwhelm, without complication, and without losing the joy of the mission.

The Principle: Duplication > Solo Effort

You've probably already had someone ask you:

"How did you do that?"
"Where did you get that deck?"
"Could I share these too?"

That's your signal.

Every time someone asks you how they can do what you're doing, that's not just a compliment—it's *an invitation to duplicate.*

You can't be everywhere. You can't talk to everyone.

But when you train a few others to do what you've done?

Suddenly… you're multiplying your income and your mission without burning out.

That's what building a team is about. And this isn't just theory—it's *scriptural.*

Jesus didn't do everything Himself. He sent the 72. Paul mentored Timothy. The early church spread through teams, homes, and shared models.

This isn't sales training.

This is **Kingdom-building.**

How to Start Building a Mutual Success Team

Here's how to begin with confidence and grace.

Step 1: Identify 2–3 People Who Are Curious or Encouraged
Start with those who:

- Already bought a deck and loved it
- Asked how you're doing this
- Are looking for extra income with purpose
- Would thrive with community support

Don't start with strangers. Start with those already near your circle.

Step 2: Share the Bigger Vision
Let them know this isn't just a product. It's a *mission + method + model.*

You can say:

"I'm not just selling these—I'm building a small team to help others do the same, with encouragement and real income."

Show them how simple it is:

- Share a few decks
- Use the method that fits their life
- Keep God at the center

Step 3: Give Them a Simple On-Ramp
Offer to:

- Help them get their first deck
- Share your favorite starting script
- Check in after their first week to encourage and celebrate

That's it.

You're not managing.

You're *mentoring.*

How This Turns Into Long-Term Income

When one of your team members sells a deck, they get income—and you get *override income*. That means a portion of their sales (or a referral bonus) comes back to you as the leader.

This creates:

- Income without extra effort
- Motivation to *help your team succeed* (not compete)
- Stability, as even small teams can produce consistent flow

Now imagine this:

- You have 5 people on your team
- Each sells just 10 decks per month
- You earn $5 from each deck sold by your team

That's $250/month in *passive income*—before you sell a single deck yourself.

And that's just the beginning.

If those team members train others... now you've got a second layer of multiplication.

This is where you shift from chasing sales... to *building systems* that serve you and your community long-term.

What to Provide Your Team (So You're Not Always "On")

You don't have to be on call 24/7.

A great team system runs on **simple resources + consistent encouragement.**

Here's what to prepare once and reuse:

1. A short welcome message

"Here's why I started sharing decks and how I got my first few sales."

2. Your favorite 1–2 methods
Show them what worked for you. Keep it clear. One paragraph each.

3. A few conversation starters or templates
Let them copy what you've already seen work. This saves hours of stress for them.

4. A place to celebrate small wins
Start a group chat or email thread where people can share what's working.

5. A monthly Zoom call or prayer chat (optional)
This deepens team connection—and keeps people inspired without chasing them down.

If you give your team these five tools, they'll feel **equipped—not overwhelmed.**

And equipped people keep going.

What Happens Over Time (When You Stay Consistent)

If you stay in motion, even modestly—here's what begins to happen over a few months:

- **Your personal sales continue** at a steady pace
- **Your team's sales increase**, even if each person stays small
- **You become a source of wisdom** for those just starting
- **You're earning even when you rest**, travel, or focus on other callings
- **People you helped... begin helping others**

That's legacy.

That's fruit that *remains.*

And that's the power of building something with systems, with people, and with purpose.

You Don't Need a Big Team—Just a Strong One

You're not trying to become a manager.

You're trying to *build mutual success.*

A small, strong team of 3–7 people can create:

- Monthly recurring income
- Encouraging culture
- Sustainable Kingdom impact
- A support system that keeps you going when life gets hard

That's what this model was designed for.

So don't worry about going viral.

Focus on going **faithful.**

Start with a few. Lead with care. Duplicate what's already working.

And soon, you'll realize...

You're no longer working *in* your business.

You're building something that works *for you—and others.* Together.

Chapter 31 – Building Your Community – Part 1: Find Others, Connect Deeply, and Grow Together

This was never meant to be a solo journey. Real success comes when we build with others, not just for ourselves.

Success grows faster when it's shared.

One of the most overlooked strategies for business—and for life—is also the most powerful: *community*.

You can have a great product, a strong message, and a clear method. But if you're walking alone, momentum will always feel harder. You'll second-guess your direction. You'll get stuck in your own head. You'll wonder if you're doing enough, or doing it right.

But the moment you connect with others—others who believe in the mission, who are walking the same path—you discover something beautiful: *you're not alone*.

That's what this chapter is about.

Because Christian Decks was never designed to be a product-only journey. It was always meant to be a *community-based calling*. That's why we encourage forming Mutual Success Teams. That's why we focus on building together.

This chapter will show you how to:

- Find others on the same path
- Share stories and strategies
- Strengthen one another in faith and encouragement
- Multiply success without competing

This is the heart of Team Success.

It's not just about selling cards. It's about *doing it together*—and going farther because of it.

Step 1: Find Your People—Start with What You Already Have

You don't need a big network. You just need a few open doors.

Here's how to start finding your Scripture Deck community:

1. Reach out to the person who introduced you.
If someone shared the deck with you, start by reconnecting. Ask:

"Are you part of a team or group using these?"
"Do you know others who are sharing this too?"

2. Ask your team leader or upline.
If you're part of a larger Mutual Success Team, they may already have:

- A group chat
- A Facebook group
- A weekly encouragement email
- A list of others you can connect with

3. Join or start a small circle.
Find 2–3 other sellers and start something simple:

- A prayer group
- A once-a-week check-in
- A "what's working" thread via group text

You don't need to wait for someone else to build it.

You can *start community* just by asking:

"Would you want to grow together and swap ideas once a week?"

Most people say yes—because they're craving it, too.

Step 2: Build a Culture of Encouragement, Not Comparison

When Christians work together, the enemy's #1 tactic is comparison.

You'll be tempted to look at someone else's numbers, social media following, or results—and shrink back. You'll tell yourself you're behind. That you're not gifted enough. That this isn't for you.

Stop right there.

Team Success works because we choose *mutual celebration, not silent competition.*

If someone has success, that's proof it's possible—not proof you're behind.

So instead of comparing, ask:

- "What did you try that worked?"
- "Would you be open to sharing your method?"
- "Could we partner and try something together?"

This creates a culture of *growth and generosity*.

And that culture will carry you through the hard days.

Because when your community is filled with celebration and wisdom-sharing, no one gets left behind.

Step 3: Share What's Working—Even If It's Small

You don't need to wait until you're an "expert" to speak up.

One of the fastest ways to create value in a community is by *sharing what you just learned.*

Try this rhythm:

- Each week, share one thing you tried
- One thing that worked
- And one thing you're still figuring out

That's it.

Example:

"I shared a card with a coworker who's been going through a lot—didn't expect much, but she said it made her cry. I realized it's not about saying the perfect thing. It's just about being available."

Or:

"I posted once on Instagram with no results, but when I added a story about why the verse mattered to me, someone DM'd asking how to get a deck."

These aren't tips from gurus.

They're *life-tested moments* that help the whole group learn and grow.

What's obvious to you might be a breakthrough to someone else.

So share.

You're not boasting.

You're *building.*

Step 4: Multiply Success Through Shared Tools

Once your community gets into a rhythm, you can go even further by **sharing tools, templates, and systems**.

This doesn't need to be complex. Just ask:

- "Would anyone be open to sharing their flyer or message template?"
- "Does anyone have a quick tutorial or intro they use?"
- "Would it help if we made a list of conversation starters together?"

When one person creates something useful—**everyone benefits.**

That's the power of collaboration.

You save time. You build faster. You encourage innovation.

And no one has to reinvent the wheel.

This is what the early church did.

They shared everything—from food to letters to spiritual gifts.

And because of that, *"there was no need among them."*

We're here to do the same.

This Is the Heartbeat of Team Success

You don't have to be perfect.

You just have to be **present**.

You don't need to have it all figured out.

You just need to be **willing to walk with others.**

Scripture Decks were never meant to be a business you do in isolation. They were designed to spark a new kind of *shared success*—one that strengthens your faith, your finances, and your friendships all at once.

So reach out.

Invite someone in.

Join a team. Start a thread. Host a prayer call. Share your story.

Because when we grow together—we grow *better*.

And when we put the Kingdom first... we all rise. Together.

Chapter 32 – Building Your Community – Part 2: Support Systems That Keep Everyone Thriving

You don't just need a team—you need a culture. A support structure. A rhythm that fuels everyone, not just the few.

So you've found your people. Now, how do you help them grow?

Once a community begins to form—whether it's two people or twenty—there's a shift. You're no longer just helping others *start*. You're helping them *stay steady*. You're building something deeper than sales. You're shaping a shared culture.

And here's the truth: *growth without support eventually breaks down.*

That's why this chapter is all about structure—not the rigid kind, but the life-giving kind. The kind that makes everyone feel seen, energized, and equipped to keep going, even when life gets busy.

You'll learn:

- How to create simple rhythms that nourish your group
- How to lead or host a local team (without pressure)
- How to build communication channels that actually serve
- How to create systems of encouragement that people want to stay part of

If you've ever said, "I want to help others, but I don't want to burn out," this chapter was made for you.

Let's show you how to build *sustainable community*—the kind that multiplies.

Step 1: Establish a Rhythm Everyone Can Rely On

The strongest communities have one thing in common: **consistency.**

You don't need daily meetings. You don't need long phone calls. You just need *a repeatable rhythm* your people can count on.

Here are three easy formats:

1. Weekly Text Check-In
Send 2–3 questions in a group chat:

- What's one win this week?
- What's something you're trying?
- How can we pray for you?

2. Bi-Weekly Encouragement Call (Zoom or in-person)
Keep it to 30 minutes. Start with prayer. Let 2–3 people share what's working. End with a scripture and one takeaway.

3. Monthly Meet-Up or "Deck & Coffee"
Host a local coffee catch-up, bring decks to show or swap ideas, and use it as a time of friendship and refreshing.

The format doesn't matter as much as the *reliability.*

Let your group know: *this happens whether two show up or twenty.*

That's how community becomes stable.

Step 2: Create Support Roles So It's Not All on You

Here's where many new leaders struggle: they try to carry *everything.*

But if this is truly a **Mutual Success Team**, then mutual support is essential.

So as your group grows, invite others into small roles. Not titles. Not pressure. Just pieces of support.

Examples:

- **The Encourager:** Sends one uplifting message each week
- **The Tech Helper:** Manages the group chat or call link

- **The Note Taker:** Captures good ideas and shares a recap
- **The Prayer Anchor:** Kicks off every meeting with a short prayer
- **The Story Sharer:** Reminds the group of one recent testimony each month

When people share the load, *they grow, too.*

They don't just attend your community. They *belong to it.*

And when ownership increases, burnout disappears.

Step 3: Use Group Messaging Channels That Fit Your People

Communication is the lifeblood of support.

But if it's scattered, stressful, or hard to find—it won't serve your group.

Here are a few tested messaging tools:

- **WhatsApp or GroupMe:** Great for ongoing conversation and quick shares
- **Email Threads:** Good for monthly check-ins or longer stories
- **Facebook Group (Private):** Ideal for photo updates, questions, and announcements
- **Text Chains:** Great for small teams or offline-focused sellers

- **Telegram or Voxer:** Helpful for audio encouragement or voice notes

Pro Tip: Choose one platform—and commit to it. Don't try to juggle three.

The goal is to make your team say: *"I love checking in here."*

Once they trust the channel, they'll show up more.

Step 4: Build Encouragement Into Your Culture (Automatically)

When life gets tough, encouragement is what keeps people going.

That's why support can't be an afterthought—it needs to be part of your group's *design*.

Here's how to make it effortless:

1. Set a Group Tone:
Let everyone know: "This space is for celebrating, not comparing. We're here to help each other win."

2. Create a Shared Wins Thread:
Have a place where anyone can drop a victory:

"I gave away my first deck!"
"I got a yes after 3 no's!"
"My teenager asked to read a card together!"

3. Schedule "Highlight Spotlights":
Once a week, highlight one person's breakthrough.

"This week's story: Susan shared with her first church and already got 5 orders!"

4. Ask, "Who Needs a Boost?"
Be honest about hard weeks. Invite people to share prayer needs or discouragement—and then respond.

These small things keep the emotional engine running.

Because when people feel *seen and supported*, they keep going.

Step 5: Start Local—And Let It Grow Naturally

Local support is powerful. When people can meet face-to-face, share decks, pray in person—it deepens the bond.

If you feel led, here's how to start:

1. Host a Deck Gathering
Invite 3–5 people for coffee or lunch. Share stories. Show cards. Let everyone talk freely.

2. Offer a "Local Launch Kit"
Print out flyers, give decks to test, and help someone get started near you.

3. Create a Regional Chat or Email List
Once you meet others nearby, make it easy to keep in touch.

4. Meet Quarterly for Worship + Strategy
Blend spiritual encouragement with business check-ins. Keep it light. Keep it life-giving.

You don't have to scale fast.

You just have to *be present.*

Start with a few people who believe—and build outward.

The Real Secret to a Thriving Community? Shared Purpose.

Every community needs a "why."

For us, it's clear:

- To spread the Word of God through simple, tangible tools
- To encourage others with daily truth
- To create financial overflow that supports Kingdom work
- To build teams where "there is no need among them"

When your group sees that shared purpose—*they stick around.*

They don't just show up. They *own the mission.*

And they're not just there for results.

They're there because they found something real.

That's the power of a well-supported, well-loved, purpose-driven Mutual Success Team.

And now... you get to build one.

Part 6: The Templates – For Leading Your Team

Once your project grows, others will want to join you. And when that happens, leadership matters. This section gives you plug-and-play templates to lead your Mutual Success Team like a pro.

You'll get a weekly meeting agenda, goal-setting worksheets, celebration event plans, and even an annual retreat guide. These tools take the guesswork out of leading—and give you the structure to build something that lasts.

Whether you're mentoring two people or twenty, these templates help you create consistency. They foster trust, encourage growth, and keep your team focused on what matters most.

Best of all, you won't need to reinvent the wheel. You'll simply apply what's here—and lead with confidence and clarity.

Chapter 33 – Weekly Meeting Agenda (Provided Template)

A simple rhythm keeps your Mutual Success Team focused, fueled, and flourishing—without extra stress.

Consistency builds trust—and trust builds momentum.

If you've ever led a group (or even just tried to keep one going), you know the biggest challenge isn't passion. It's *pacing.*

People start strong—but life gets busy. Weeks go by. Enthusiasm fades. And what once felt electric... starts to fizzle.

But it doesn't have to be that way.

In fact, one of the most powerful things you can do for your Mutual Success Team is create a **weekly rhythm**—a short, focused, life-giving meeting that keeps everyone aligned, encouraged, and moving forward.

This chapter gives you exactly that.

Not just ideas. A template.

Because the truth is: meetings don't have to be long to be meaningful.

You just need a few minutes each week—anchored in Scripture, wins, prayer, and strategy—to keep your team strong and your vision clear.

Let's break it down.

Why Weekly Meetings Work (Even at 10 Minutes Long)

You don't need hour-long Zooms or complicated check-ins. A short, intentional meeting creates:

- **Rhythm** – Something steady to look forward to
- **Accountability** – A reason to keep going and show up
- **Encouragement** – A chance to share wins and lift each other up
- **Direction** – Space to ask questions and swap strategies
- **Faith** – A spiritual reminder that this is *God's work*, not just business

This one weekly touchpoint helps prevent isolation, burnout, confusion, and comparison.

It helps your team feel supported and connected—even when everyone's busy.

And when people feel supported? *They stay in motion.*

How to Host the Weekly Meeting

Where:

- Group text thread (via voice memo or typed)
- Zoom or Google Meet (great for face-to-face)
- In-person at a coffee shop, kitchen table, or church lobby
- Audio message via Voxer or Telegram if your team prefers asynchronous

When:
Pick a consistent day and time. Example:

"Every Tuesday at 7pm PST"
"Every Sunday afternoon via group text"
"Every Monday morning—audio recap in group chat"

Let your team know it's okay to miss—but consistency is what *builds the habit*.

Who leads it?
Rotate! You don't always have to be "the leader." Let others take turns reading a verse, praying, or guiding discussion.

Recommended Weekly Meeting Agenda (10–20 minutes)

Here's the full agenda template you can copy, save, and start using this week.

📝 **Mutual Success Team – Weekly Meeting Agenda**

Estimated Time: 10–20 minutes
(Adjust for in-person or online)

---

1. Opening Prayer (1–2 mins)
Ask one person to open in prayer, inviting God to lead the meeting and strengthen each member.

2. Scripture of the Week (2 mins)
Choose one card from the Scripture Deck. Read it aloud. Ask:

"How does this speak to where you're at this week?"
Give 1–2 people time to respond briefly.

3. Celebrate the Wins (3–5 mins)
Ask:

"What's one win this week—big or small?"
It could be:

- A conversation with someone
- A deck sold or gifted

- A step taken, even if it didn't "work"
- A personal insight from trying something new

4. Strategy Round (5–7 mins)
Ask:

"What's working for you right now?"
"Any methods or messages that got good responses?"
"What would you try differently next time?"

This creates *shared learning*. One person's small breakthrough could help the whole team.

Optional: Recap a helpful section from a previous chapter to review a proven approach.

5. Ask for Support (2–3 mins)
Invite anyone to share:

"What do you need help with this week?"
It might be:

- A prayer request
- An idea to try
- Encouragement or accountability

Let the group speak into it.

6. Set the Intention (1 min)
Everyone says one sentence:

"This week, I will ________."
Examples:

- "Follow up with three people."
- "Post my favorite verse online."
- "Host my first deck gathering."
- "Rest and trust God while planting seeds."

7. Closing Prayer (1–2 mins)
Ask a second person to pray over the week ahead—blessing every team member, conversation, and opportunity.

□ Post-Meeting Optional Follow-Up

- Share a quick summary in the chat (1–2 takeaways)
- Highlight someone's win
- Remind the group: "Same time next week!"

Bonus: Tools to Make It Smoother

Use any of the following to support your rhythm:

- **Meeting Reminder Template (text):**

"Hey team! 15 mins until our Weekly Encouragement Chat. Bring a card to share & a win if you've got one ☺"

- **Card of the Week Graphic:**
  Use Canva to create a visual each week from your deck to spark discussion.
- **Prayer Thread:**
  Create a permanent space for ongoing requests throughout the week.
- **Shared Resources Folder:**
  Keep files like flyer templates, scripts, and photos in a shared Google Drive or Dropbox.

These light systems add structure without stress.

Keep It Human. Keep It Holy. Keep It Weekly.

You don't need to be perfect.
You don't need to be profound.
You just need to *show up together*.

That's how movements begin.

These weekly meetings might seem small—but over time, they become sacred. They hold people up. They rekindle purpose. They remind everyone: *You're not doing this alone.*

So print the template. Set a time. Invite two people.

And begin.

Because weekly rhythms don't just sustain your team.

They **build your future**—one faithful meeting at a time.

Chapter 34 – Monthly Goal Setting (Provided Worksheets)

Goals aren't pressure—they're permission. A clear target helps you aim with purpose, stay encouraged, and celebrate what's really working.

You don't drift into financial success. You decide your way there.

One of the biggest breakthroughs for any Scripture Deck seller is the moment they stop "hoping it works" and start *intentionally planning what they want to see happen.*

This doesn't mean rigid hustle.

It doesn't mean putting pressure on yourself.

It simply means creating *clarity*—and choosing to live your next month on purpose.

This chapter walks you through how to set monthly goals that:

- Fit your season of life

- Keep your heart encouraged
- Align with your faith
- Lead to real income and impact

You'll also receive two practical tools:

- **Monthly Personal Goal Planner**
- **Monthly Mutual Success Team Tracker**

Use these worksheets every 30 days. They'll help you reflect, refocus, and refresh your mission—one step at a time.

Let's break down how to use them and why they work.

Why Monthly Goals Work Better Than Daily Stress

It's tempting to focus on "doing more each day." But that often leads to burnout. We get discouraged when we miss one day—and spiral into guilt or inaction.

Monthly goals are different.

They give you:

- **Breathing room** to adjust and adapt
- **Big-picture clarity** to focus on what really matters
- **Momentum tracking** you can look back on with gratitude

A 30-day window is long enough to see fruit, but short enough to course-correct fast.

That's why we recommend this rhythm:

- **Set your goals once per month (Day 1)**
- **Check your progress once per week (10-minute check-in)**
- **Celebrate and reset at month-end**

This keeps the mission light, consistent, and *doable.*

Now let's explore the two key worksheets that support this.

Worksheet 1: Monthly Personal Goal Planner

This worksheet is for *you*—as an individual seller or leader. It helps you define what you're aiming for, how you plan to get there, and how you want to grow spiritually along the way.

📓 Monthly Personal Goal Planner

Use this at the beginning of each month (or 30-day period)

1. My Monthly Vision
In one or two sentences, describe what success would feel like this month.

"I want to help 10 people get encouraged with the Word and create $500 in income to support my family."

---

2. My Core Scripture for the Month

Choose a verse from your deck that anchors your mindset this month.

"I chose Philippians 4:13 – I can do all things through Christ who gives me strength."

---

3. This Month I Will…

✓ Share the deck with ___ new people

✓ Sell or gift ___ total decks

✓ Post or share about Scripture ___ times

✓ Invite ___ people to join my team

✓ Spend ___ minutes/week in focused Scripture & planning time

✓ Host ___ local or online meet-ups (optional)

---

4. What's Working from Last Month

What methods or moments brought momentum last month?

"Every time I shared a personal story, people responded. My coffee shop convo led to 2 sales."

---

5. Where I Need Growth or Support

What felt hard, unclear, or frustrating last month?

"I procrastinated outreach because I didn't feel confident with what to say."

---

6. My Encouragement Plan

☐ Ask someone to check in with me weekly

☐ Celebrate one win each Friday

☐ Write down every "yes" AND every "no"—they both count as progress

☐ Give God the outcome, not just the effort

---

7. My One-Line Monthly Declaration

Write a sentence to keep in front of you all month.

"God is with me. I'm planting seeds in faith. I succeed by showing up."

📌 *Put this planner somewhere visible—on your desk, wall, or in your journal.*

Worksheet 2: Monthly Mutual Success Team Tracker

This worksheet is for group leaders or team builders. It helps you support your team, track collective wins, and plan support strategies that strengthen the whole network.

📓 Monthly Mutual Success Team Tracker

Fill this out with your group or leadership circle once a month

1. Team Name or Region:

---

2. Team Vision for the Month
What's our shared mission this month?

"We want every person to share with at least 3 people and help the group grow by 5 new decks total."

---

3. Scripture that Guides Our Team This Month:

"Let us not grow weary in doing good…" – Galatians 6:9

---

4. Total Team Goals (This Month)

- ✓ ___ total decks sold
- ✓ ___ new team members added
- ✓ ___ people encouraged with the Word
- ✓ ___ methods tried and documented
- ✓ ___ meetings or check-ins completed

---

5. Member Highlights

What's one win or story from each member?

- Susan: Sold 3 decks at her Bible study
- David: Invited his cousin to join the team
- Erica: Shared a card with her Uber driver and sparked a powerful convo

---

6. What We Learned This Month

List top 3 takeaways:

1. ______________________
2. ______________________
3. ______________________

---

7. Support Strategy (Next Month)

How will we support our team better?

☐ Weekly prayer chain

☐ Video testimony night
☐ Local "Deck Party" event
☐ Add a new resource or flyer
☐ Mentorship pairings for encouragement

---

8. Our Monthly Team Declaration

"Together we grow. Together we give. Together we go forward in faith and overflow."

📌 *Review this together at your next team meeting.*

How to Make These Worksheets a Habit

- Print and use them every 30 days
- Keep them in a folder, binder, or Google Drive
- Share in your group or ask your team to submit their version (if they want)
- Use them as prompts in weekly meetings
- Set a recurring calendar reminder on your phone: "New Month Goal Setting – 30 minutes"

Goal Setting + Faith = Peaceful Progress

These worksheets aren't about pressure. They're not about performance.

They're about *showing up on purpose*—and trusting God to bless your faithfulness.

As you use these tools, you'll begin to notice:

- Your confidence increasing
- Your conversations flowing more naturally
- Your team feeling more connected
- Your income and impact growing with clarity

Because what you focus on *multiplies.*

So focus this next month on:

- What matters most
- What you can control
- And who God is calling you to bless

And watch what He does with your intentionality.

Chapter 35 – Quarterly Celebrations (Provided Event Plans)

We're not just building businesses. We're building family. And family celebrates together.

When God moves—celebrate it. When people grow—honor it. When the mission advances—mark the moment.

That's what this chapter is all about.

In the early church, there was no separation between mission and joy. The believers gathered "with glad and sincere hearts" (Acts 2:46). They broke bread. They praised God. They witnessed miracles—and *celebrated the movement together.*

We're bringing that same spirit into our Mutual Success Teams.

Because success in the Kingdom isn't cold or corporate. It's *communal*. It's *celebratory*. It's about people, presence, and progress—together.

That's why every 3 months, we recommend holding a **Quarterly Celebration**. These are not just events. They are **anchors**. They give your team something to look forward to, a reason to pause, and a moment to mark how far you've come.

This chapter will walk you through:

- Why celebrations multiply results
- How to structure your quarterly events
- What elements create energy and unity
- 3 ready-to-use event templates (adaptable for in-person or online)

Let's build gatherings that are full of joy, focused on growth, and formed around faith.

Why Quarterly Celebrations Matter

Most people don't quit because they don't care.

They quit because they feel *alone*... or because they forget how far they've come.

Quarterly celebrations fix that.

They:

- Remind people of their progress
- Increase team loyalty and unity
- Refresh vision for the next quarter

- Create a culture of gratitude and momentum
- Spark new stories and breakthroughs

These events don't have to be large or flashy.

They just need to be *intentional.*

And they're not just for your current team—they're for everyone who needs to see that Mutual Success is *real and alive.*

Essential Elements of a Great Celebration

Whether you're hosting five people in your living room or fifty people on Zoom, every celebration needs these four elements:

1. Story Sharing
Testimonies are the heartbeat. Let people share what God has done through the Scripture Decks, their personal growth, or their income breakthrough.

2. Public Honor
Shout out progress. Celebrate people by name. Give awards, prizes, or even just heartfelt praise. Recognition multiplies retention.

3. Vision Reset
Recast the mission. Remind everyone *why we do this.* Use a scripture, a story, or a visual to say: "We're just getting started."

4. Next Steps Invitation
Use the momentum to invite people to re-engage, try a new method, join a team, or mentor someone else.

These ingredients create connection—and keep people coming back.

🎉 Event Plan 1: "Quarterly Celebration Night" (In-Person or Zoom)

Ideal For:

- Local Mutual Success Teams
- Regional gatherings
- Online teams needing reconnection

Length: 60–90 minutes

A. Welcome & Prayer (5 mins)

- Start with energy and gratitude
- Open in prayer and set the tone: "We're here to honor God and each other."

B. Story Highlights (20 mins)

- Let 3–5 people share their top moment this quarter:

"What's something that happened because you said yes to this mission?"
"What impact did the Scripture Deck have in your world?"

C. Recognition Time (15 mins)
Use fun categories like:

- Most Encouraging Teammate
- First Deck Sold
- Quiet Hero (someone who showed up behind the scenes)
- Breakthrough Moment
- Best Recovery from Rejection

Give printable awards, small gifts, or just speak honor.

D. Worship Moment (Optional – 5–10 mins)
If in person, use live acoustic worship. If on Zoom, play a recorded song and invite people to reflect or pray silently.

E. Vision Message (10 mins)
Recast the purpose. Use slides or a short story to remind the team:

"We're building something eternal. This is how we change lives."

F. Next Quarter Preview (10 mins)

- Share what's coming up:

"New deck themes..."
"Upcoming team trainings..."
"Goal: 100 new people reached with the Word"

G. Group Photo & Closing Prayer (5 mins)
Capture the moment. End with a blessing over each person's next step.

🎉 Event Plan 2: "Deck & Dinner Night" (Local Celebration)

Ideal For:

- Smaller in-home teams
- Church-based teams
- Fellowship-focused groups

Length: 2 hours

A. Food & Fellowship (45 mins)

- Potluck or pizza night
- Everyone brings a dish or drink
- Decks on the table for anyone to flip through

B. Testimony Circle (30 mins)

- Sit in a circle
- Each person shares one win or moment of encouragement

"This deck helped me..."
"I finally felt confident when I..."

C. Encouragement Card Swap (10 mins)

- Each person picks one card from the deck
- Writes a note to someone else with that verse
- Exchanges the encouragement

D. Group Prayer & Declaration (15 mins)

- Read a scripture out loud (e.g., Romans 12:10)
- Pray for one another
- Speak this together:

"We are blessed to be a blessing. We are called and equipped. This quarter, we go forward in unity."

E. Share a Next Step (10 mins)

- Each person says:

"Next quarter, I plan to..."

- Write it down and exchange with a buddy to check in later

🎉 Event Plan 3: "Zoom Impact Rally" (Online Celebration)

Ideal For:

- Multi-state or international teams
- Digital-first networks
- Large groups that can't meet locally

Length: 60 minutes

A. Host Welcome (5 mins)

- Energetic greeting
- Invite everyone to drop their city or favorite card in the chat

B. 3 Impact Stories (15 mins)

- Choose 3 people to share ahead of time
- Focus on transformation:

"This mission helped me…"
"My deck opened the door for…"

C. Recognition Spotlight (10 mins)

- Highlight 5–10 people

- Use slides with names and short comments like:

  "Faithful encourager."
  "Creative outreach idea."
  "Biggest breakthrough."

D. Team Training Nugget (10 mins)

- Share one new method, tip, or tool
- Keep it practical:

  "Here's how I started a small booth..."
  "What worked best on social media..."

E. Vision Reset (10 mins)

- Share team-wide goals
- Preview next training or event
- Show the big picture: "Together, we're reaching hundreds with God's Word."

F. Group Prayer & Charge (5 mins)

- Close with a unifying prayer
- Speak this together:

"We are a Mutual Success Team. And we are just getting started."

Tips to Make Celebrations Easy and Impactful

- **Assign roles ahead of time** – Don't carry it all. Let someone host, another pray, someone else share a win.
- **Keep it light** – Smiles go farther than spreadsheets.
- **Document it** – Take photos or record videos to use for next time.
- **Send a recap email** – Share highlights and keep the fire burning.
- **Honor the quiet ones** – Celebrate effort, not just results.

Quarterly Celebrations = Long-Term Culture

This isn't just about marking time.

It's about building *team memory*.

When people look back and say:

"Remember that night we prayed together?"
"Remember when she told her story and we all cried?"
"Remember when we hit that team goal?"

Those memories become *anchors*.

They keep people through the hard months. They connect teammates across distance. They spark joy, gratitude, and fuel to go again.

So mark the calendar.

Set the rhythm.

Honor the journey.

Because in the Kingdom—we don't just reach milestones.

We celebrate *faithfulness*.

And then, we *go again*.

Chapter 36 – Annual Vision Renewal (Provided Retreat Guide)

You don't just need goals. You need grounding. An annual retreat gives you the pause that reveals your next leap.

Every mission needs a moment to breathe.

After a year of planting seeds, trying strategies, and building something real—it's easy to lose track of *why* you started, *where* you're going, and *what* God is still calling you toward.

That's why we created the **Annual Vision Renewal Retreat**.

It's not just a review. It's a *reset*—a spiritual, mental, emotional, and practical space where you step out of routine and into renewal.

This isn't about pressure. It's about peace.

It's not about fixing anything. It's about *remembering everything.*

In this chapter, you'll get a complete retreat guide—designed for:

- Individuals (doing a solo retreat)
- Local or regional Mutual Success Teams
- Team leaders and trainers
- Church-affiliated project teams

The format is simple. The outcome is profound.

Because when you give God one day of full attention—*He often gives you a year of clear direction.*

Let's walk through what this annual retreat can look like for you.

□ What is the Annual Vision Renewal Retreat?

It's a 1-day, 2-day, or weekend experience that helps you:

- Reflect on what's happened
- Reconnect with your "why"
- Realign with God's voice
- Refocus on your next season
- Receive rest, healing, and fresh clarity

This retreat can be hosted:

- In-person (in a home, church, cabin, or conference space)
- Online (via Zoom for remote teams)

- Solo (at a prayer cabin, hotel room, or your own living space)

There is no perfect format—only *intentional presence.*

📋 Annual Vision Renewal Retreat Guide

Use this guide to plan and lead a complete retreat—whether for yourself or your team.

✨ **RETREAT OVERVIEW**

Title:
Annual Vision Renewal Retreat – "See Again. Believe Again. Begin Again."

Ideal Length:

- Solo: 1 full day or 2 half-days
- Team: 2 days (Friday evening – Saturday night)

Supplies Needed:

- Journal or print-out of included worksheets
- Bible and your Scripture Deck
- Comfortable setting (quiet if possible)

- Optional: candles, worship playlist, coffee/tea, blankets, markers

---

DAY 1: Reflect, Release, Remember

Session 1: Quiet Arrival + Worship (30 min)

- Play soft worship or instrumental music
- Settle in. Breathe. Pray slowly.
- Read Psalm 23 or Isaiah 43 aloud

Prompt:

"God, thank You for what You've brought me through. I give You this retreat. Speak to me. I'm listening."

Session 2: The Year in Review (1 hour)
Worksheet A – "The Year That Was"

Answer the following in writing:

1. What were the biggest wins this year?
2. What surprised me?
3. What did I overcome?
4. Where did I grow in faith, courage, or leadership?
5. What didn't go as expected?
6. What did I learn about God, myself, and others?

Take your time. Then pray:

"Thank You for the journey. I give You what didn't work. I treasure what did. And I release it all back to You."

Session 3: Share the Story (30–60 min, if with team)

- Break into pairs or small groups
- Share 1–2 powerful stories from the year
- Ask:

"What story will I carry into next year as a testimony?"

End with celebration and prayer for each person.

🔥 **DAY 2: Realign, Refocus, Reignite**

Session 4: The Why Behind It All (1 hour)
Worksheet B – "My Mission Reminders"

Write down:

- Why did I begin this?
- Who am I doing this for?
- What scripture anchors my work?
- What testimony reminds me it's worth it?
- What do I need to remember more often?

End by holding a card from your deck that represents your why. Read it aloud.

Session 5: Casting Fresh Vision (1.5 hours)
Worksheet C – "What's Next: My Vision for This Year"

Reflect and write:

- This year, I believe God is calling me to...
- I want to reach ___ people with the Word
- I want to mentor ___ people into this mission
- I want to earn $___ (goal) to support my family and mission
- I want to create:

  ☐ A new team
  ☐ A new deck
  ☐ A new training
  ☐ A new partnership
  ☐ Other: ____________

Draw your vision if helpful. Use colored markers or make a visual map. Be creative.

Session 6: Strategic Planning with God (1 hour)
Worksheet D – "My 3-Part Game Plan"

1. **SPIRIT:**
   What will keep my soul strong this year?
   ☐ Weekly scripture rhythm
   ☐ Mutual Success prayer calls
   ☐ Rest rhythms
   ☐ Other: ___________
2. **SYSTEM:**
   What structure will keep me consistent?
   ☐ Weekly check-in
   ☐ Monthly goal planner
   ☐ Quarterly celebration plan
   ☐ Other: ___________
3. **SUCCESS:**
   What will success *feel like* this year?
   ☐ Peace
   ☐ Overflow
   ☐ Team growth
   ☐ Impact stories
   ☐ Other: ___________

Close this session by declaring:

"Lord, I give You my plan—and invite You to lead it."

Session 7: Prophetic Prayer + Group Vision Speak (1 hour)
If hosting a team retreat:

- Let 2–3 leaders pray over every person

- Share words of encouragement or vision
- Let each person speak a declaration aloud for the year

"This year, I believe God will..."
"I will grow in..."
"Our team will see..."

Close in worship or group communion if appropriate.

Final Reflection: Quiet Sending (30 min)

Sit in silence for 5–10 minutes.

Then write:

- What did I hear God whisper this weekend?
- What is my word for the year?
- What is one action I will take in the next 7 days?

"Thank You, Lord, for renewing my spirit. I go forward with faith, peace, and joy."

End with a group photo or a personal symbolic action (e.g., burning a note, tying a string, placing a stone on an altar of remembrance).

Optional Add-Ons for the Retreat

- Print retreat booklets with all worksheets
- Create a prayer wall or gratitude journal table
- Offer a "Quiet Walk" time outdoors
- Record video reflections from attendees to share with others
- Provide retreat gifts: a new deck, a journal, a candle

The Power of Pause: Yearly Rhythm. Lifetime Impact.

When you take time to pause and hear from God—everything changes.

You don't just come out with goals.

You come out with *clarity... courage...* and *conviction.*

You remember why this all matters.

You realize just how far you've come.

You reignite the spark that keeps you moving forward—not just for income, but for impact. For souls. For community. For the Kingdom.

So book the retreat.

Mark the calendar.

Gather your team.

Because your next breakthrough might not come from doing more—

It might come from *pausing well.*

Part 7: The Ways – Finally Pick Your Favorite Way To Sell From 100+

This is where the fun really begins. We're not giving you a business in theory—we're giving you 100+ ways to make it work in real life. This part of the book is your idea bank, your strategy vault, and your launchpad.

Whether you prefer in-person events, online strategies, ministry-based outreach, or creative gifting methods—there's a fit for you. Each idea is short, actionable, and designed to meet you where you are.

You'll learn how to test an idea in 30 days, track results, and share your findings with the Team Success Network. This builds momentum, creates breakthroughs, and connects you with others doing the same.

Don't overthink it—just pick one and start. Your next chapter of income, impact, and success may begin with one small step from this very list.

Chapter 37 – Try Your Favorite Idea for 30 Days: Experiment for a Month

What could change if you gave just 30 days of focused action? Let's find out—together.

You don't need to be perfect. You just need to start.

By this point in the journey, you've read dozens of strategies. You've seen the stories. You've felt the momentum. And somewhere along the way—an idea sparked inside you.

Maybe it was a method. A platform. A people group you care about. A way to share the cards that feels *natural to you.*

Here's what we know for sure: *That spark matters.*

But it's just a spark—until you give it fire.

That's why this chapter is your invitation. Not to think more. Not to wait more.

But to **try something. For real. For 30 days.**

Because everything changes when you start moving with purpose. You'll learn more in one month of action than in six months of planning.

So choose your favorite idea. Then **commit to 30 days of intentional focus**.

This chapter gives you the mindset, structure, and encouragement to test your path, track your growth, and share your story with the wider Team Success Network.

Let's turn your idea... into momentum.

Why 30 Days Works Better Than "Someday"

The secret to breakthrough isn't working harder.

It's *giving yourself a window.*

When you choose a 30-day experiment, a few powerful things happen:

1. **Urgency rises.** You know you've got a short runway—so you move.
2. **Procrastination falls.** It's not a lifetime commitment—just a test.
3. **Clarity increases.** You stop second-guessing and start learning.
4. **Results appear.** Even small wins stack up fast when you're focused.

Most people wait too long trying to get it perfect.

But you? You're going to *practice your way into progress.*

And after 30 days, you'll have:

- Real data
- Real stories
- Real confidence
- A system that fits *you*

You can always refine later.

But for now—*just try.*

How to Run Your 30-Day Experiment

You don't need a big launch. You just need a simple plan.

Here's how to make it work:

Step 1: Choose One Method

Pick the method that fits you best. This might be:

- Sharing in-person with family, friends, or church groups
- Posting online (Instagram, TikTok, Facebook)
- Hosting a Scripture Deck party or coffee night

- Partnering with a local store or church table
- Creating short videos of card encouragement
- Mailing decks with handwritten notes
- Starting a team of 3 and encouraging each other weekly

Whatever excites you most—*start there.*

God can multiply your favorite method when it's rooted in faith and offered in love.

Step 2: Set Simple Targets

Don't overload yourself. Just answer this:

"What would make this month feel successful to me?"

Some examples:

- Talk to 10 new people about the deck
- Share 5 cards in public settings
- Sell or gift 20 decks
- Try one event (local or online)
- Record 4 short videos
- Post 3 times a week with Scripture insights
- Invite 2 people to try selling with you

Write your goals. Keep them visible. They're not pressure—they're *permission.*

Step 3: Track with Simplicity

At the end of each day or week, ask:

- What did I try today?
- What went well?
- What did I learn?
- What would I tweak for tomorrow?

Use a journal, a phone note, or the Monthly Personal Goal Planner (from Chapter 34). The key is consistency.

Tracking keeps you anchored—even when you feel unsure.

Step 4: Stay Encouraged

This journey isn't about perfect execution. It's about *faithful movement.*

Some days you'll feel strong. Other days... distracted, busy, or uncertain.

Here's how to stay encouraged:

- Text someone on your Mutual Success Team: *"Just did my daily share!"*
- Re-read a favorite testimony
- Post a daily Scripture from your deck to keep your spirit lifted

- Schedule a weekly check-in with a friend
- Revisit your "why" when doubt creeps in

God doesn't ask you to do everything.

He asks you to *move with what's in your hand.*

And right now—you've got a deck, a story, and a mission.

Step 5: Share Your Results

This part is *crucial*.

At the end of your 30 days, no matter what happened—**share it**.

Why? Because:

- Your story will encourage someone else
- You'll process what you learned
- You'll start to see your path more clearly
- You'll inspire your team (and maybe even the world)

You can email your testimony directly to:

📨 **results@TeamSuccessNetwork.com**

Just write a few sentences:

- What idea did you try?
- What happened?

- What did you learn?
- What would you recommend to others?

Even if it didn't "work" the way you expected—it *worked*.

Because you moved. You learned. You grew.

And that's what this mission is about.

💡 What Happens After 30 Days?

Here's what often happens when people finish their first 30-day run:

✅ They realize what fits them best
✅ They find a rhythm that feels sustainable
✅ They gain boldness and peace
✅ They start mentoring others
✅ They hit income goals they thought were far away
✅ They start to see... this can actually work

Some people double down on what worked.

Others switch it up and try a new 30-day test.

The important thing is this: *They keep moving.*

Because once you see the fruit of momentum—you never want to stop.

This Is the Power of Short-Term Focus with Eternal Impact

You don't need to have everything figured out.

You just need to start with what you have, where you are, for 30 days.

God can multiply what's offered in faith.

So start now. Try your idea. Share your journey.

And remember...

Success isn't just the result of big launches.

It's the fruit of **daily obedience.**

Of seeds planted.

Of encouragement shared.

Of one card at a time... bringing God's Word into hearts and homes.

Your 30 days start now.

Let's go.

Chapter 38 – "To Our Mutual Success" Together

This isn't the end of the book. It's the beginning of your movement. And you're not doing it alone.

You've made it to the final chapter—of the beginning.

Because what we've built together in these pages is more than a guide, more than a product plan, more than a business training.

It's a shared mission. A Kingdom idea. A mutual success project, wrapped in prayer, strategy, faith, and the practical tools to *actually begin.*

We've talked about decks and dollars. Yes.

But even more—we've talked about legacy. And love. And lifting others as we go.

This is the end of the introduction...

...and the beginning of something so much bigger.

If you feel a fire stirring in your heart, that's no accident.
It's a signal.

That God is calling you.
That this mission fits you.
That now is the time to step forward.

Because you're not just holding a product. You're holding a seed.
And it was never meant to stay in your hand.

You're Not Alone in This

This next step you're about to take? You're not walking it solo.

There's a **network behind you.**
There are **teams praying for you.**
There are **methods and models already working—and being shared freely.**
There are **people who want to help you succeed.**

Because in the Mutual Success Team, your success matters.
Your story matters.
Your contribution matters.

You've joined something that **multiplies**.

Every Scripture Deck you share plants truth.

Every dollar earned can support your family *and* someone else's.

Every team member you mentor creates another wave of impact.

You're not running a business in isolation.
You're building the *Kingdom in motion.*

And that's why it works.

Your Simple Next Step

If your heart is saying "yes," but your mind's asking, *"Okay... but what do I actually do next?"* — this section is for you.

Let's keep it simple.

Here's your next step:

Choose one idea—and try it for 30 days.

That's it.

Turn the page, explore the upcoming ideas, pick *just one*, and commit to testing it for a month.

- No pressure.
- No overwhelm.
- Just one method, one effort, one move in the direction of God's call.

Then—when you've tried it—**share your story.**
Let the Team Success Network hear what worked, what didn't, and what God showed you in the process.

📨 Send it to: **results@TeamSuccessNetwork.com**

That email isn't just a collection point.

It's a spark starter. A celebration hub. A vault of real-life proof that God is moving through ordinary people—doing extraordinary things together.

Before You Turn the Page… Say This With Us

Let's seal this moment with a declaration of unity and intention.

Speak this out loud if you're ready:

"I am part of something bigger than me.
I'm choosing to walk in purpose, not pressure.
I'm building something that blesses others.
I believe God can use me, just as I am.
I say yes to movement.
I say yes to faith.
I say yes to our mutual success—together."

Pause.
Let that settle.

Feel the shift.

Because this is your moment.
This is your season.
And this is your invitation to begin—not later. Now.

To Our Mutual Success – We Mean It

This phrase isn't just a slogan.

It's a spiritual truth.
It's a strategy for impact.
It's a family code.

To Our Mutual Success means:

- We don't succeed at someone else's expense.
- We don't isolate to protect our pride.
- We share. We teach. We rise together.

In a world that says "compete," we say "complete."
In a culture that hoards, we give freely.
In a system that favors the few, we build for *everyone.*

That's what Mutual Success means.

That's what this deck, this book, this movement is about.

You've read the vision.
You've seen the plan.
Now... it's your turn to try it.

The next chapter isn't theory. It's action.

We're giving you **hundreds of ideas** to share and sell the Scripture Decks—*your way*.

Pick the one that fits.

And start building your story.

To your impact.
To your overflow.
To your bold steps of faith.

To our mutual success—together.

Chapter 39 – The 100+ Ways You Can Sell Christian Decks – Start Picking Your Favorite

An Introduction & Overview

The cards are just the beginning. The ideas are the pathway. The result is global Kingdom transformation—and your financial freedom.

Ready to change the world?

What you hold in your hands—this deck of Scripture—is powerful. It's truth in motion. It's encouragement made tangible. It's a Kingdom tool designed to inspire, uplift, and remind people of what really matters. But even more powerful than the cards themselves... are the ideas that will help you share them.

Because now, you're not just holding a product—you're stepping into a strategy.

This chapter launches you into 100+ ways to share, sell, and spread your decks—each one practical, personal, and proven to align with real-life strengths and circumstances. Whether you're starting small with family, dreaming big with digital, or somewhere in between—there's a method that fits you perfectly.

We've organized the ideas into sections—so you can find your fit, pick your starting path, and begin your journey *with confidence*. What you'll see below is just the beginning. Each section is a doorway into new connections, financial success, and Kingdom impact.

SECTION A: Personal Network Foundations

Building Team Success through Existing Relationships

This is the warmest, most natural starting point for anyone new to selling. These 20 ideas focus on family, friends, neighbors, coworkers, church members, and everyday relationships—people who already trust you. From birthday gifts to ministry connections to holiday blessings, this section helps you move gently into momentum.

You'll find ideas like:

- The Family Circle Launch
- The Church Friends Network
- The Thank You Token Strategy
- The Healthcare Heroes Strategy
- The Small Group Integration

Key Benefit: These approaches let you practice safely, get your first few sales with joy, and build a strong foundation of support. Start here if you want low-pressure success and relational confidence.

SECTION B: Church and Ministry Partnerships

Transforming Congregations into Mutual Success Communities

Here, we level up—taking your reach beyond individuals into the church world. These 20 ideas focus on pastors, youth groups, small groups, retreats, chaplains, and ministry leaders. You'll learn how to equip ministries with Scripture Decks that fund their programs *and* expand your influence.

Sample ideas include:

- The Sunday School Fundraiser Revolution
- The Youth Group Mission Trip Engine
- The Pastor Appreciation Strategy
- The Prison Ministry Outreach
- The Hospital Chaplain Partnership

Key Benefit: These methods offer recurring income, bulk sales, and long-term partnerships. If you're well-connected in ministry or want to serve churches while growing your business, this is your sweet spot.

SECTION C: Events and Seasonal Strategies

Maximizing Team Success through Community Engagement and Timing

This section shows how you can ride the wave of holidays, fairs, gift seasons, and local events. Whether you love farmer's markets or Christian music festivals, these 20 methods help you match your message to moments when people are *already* looking for meaningful gifts.

Featured ideas:

- The Craft Fair Circuit Mastery
- The Graduation Gift Campaign
- The Christmas Market Mastery

- The Back-to-School Special
- The Sports Tournament Ministry

Key Benefit: These are high-visibility, high-momentum options that often create spikes in both income and exposure. Perfect for seasonal pushes, vendor tables, and reaching new audiences fast.

SECTION D: Digital and Advanced Strategies

Leveraging Technology and Innovation for Exponential Team Success

This is where things get exciting. These 20+ ideas are for the creative, the online-savvy, and those ready to scale. From YouTube channels and blog platforms to affiliate programs and virtual reality, this section shows how Scripture Decks fit perfectly in the digital age.

Examples include:

- The Facebook Marketplace Mastery
- The TikTok Scripture Moments
- The Email Newsletter Empire
- The Digital Product Bundle
- The AI-Powered Personalization

Key Benefit: These methods are scalable, innovative, and ideal for those who want to build passive income streams or expand their reach far beyond their local area. If you want to grow online—this is your territory.

SECTION E: Advanced and Creative Strategies

Revolutionary Approaches for Extraordinary Team Success and Kingdom Impact

Ready to pioneer something bold? These advanced options involve chaplaincies, cruise ships, hospitals, celebrities, corporate gifting, and even the space program. These 20+ ideas stretch the boundaries and invite Kingdom visionaries to dream bigger than ever.

Examples include:

- The Corporate Chaplain Network
- The Real Estate Closing Gift Program
- The Disaster Relief Ministry
- The Theme Park Partnership
- The Military Base Outreach

Key Benefit: These ideas carry large-scale impact, media potential, and powerful partnership opportunities. If you're thinking big—and willing to build systems—this is your chapter.

Retail & Government Bonus Categories

Scripture in Stores and Service

We've also included dozens of specialized ideas in:

- **Retail Revolution** – Big box stores, pop-ups, subscription boxes, wholesale networks
- **Government & Military** – VA partnerships, police and fire chaplaincies, congressional and Coast Guard ministry

These bonus ideas round out the full 118 and offer institutional pathways for those called to work in official and structured environments.

What's Next? Your Yes.

You don't need all 100+ ideas.

You just need one that fits.

And once you try it, it will work.

Because Scripture always works. And when paired with love, strategy, and the support of your Mutual Success Team—you're unstoppable.

The cards are just the beginning.
The ideas are the pathway.
The result? A life of purpose, peace, and overflow.

So turn the page... and pick your favorite.

CHAPTER 40 – 100+ Ideas - To Sell Christian Decks

"Choose Your Idea, Change Your Life"

"There are many ways to build the Kingdom, but they all require taking the first step. Find the method that resonates with your heart, matches your situation, and aligns with your calling. Your Mutual Success Team begins with your first yes."

SECTION A: PERSONAL NETWORK FOUNDATIONS

Building Team Success Through Existing Relationships

Idea 1: The Family Circle Launch

"Start Where Love Lives"

The Approach: Begin with immediate family members who want to see you succeed and will purchase cards to support your new venture, even before they fully understand the product.

Why It Works: Family relationships provide the safest environment to practice your presentation, build confidence, and generate initial sales momentum. Your relatives are emotionally invested in your success and will often become your best advocates.

"Team Success" Application: Family members often become your first Mutual Success Team members when they see how the cards impact their own spiritual lives and witness your early success.

Idea 2: The Church Friends Network

"Leveraging Spiritual Relationships"

The Approach: Connect with fellow church members who already know your character and share your faith values, positioning Scripture cards as tools for mutual spiritual growth and practical blessing.

Why It Works: Church friendships are built on shared values and mutual support. These relationships naturally embrace faith-based products and understand the spiritual significance of Scripture memorization and gift-giving.

"Team Success" Application: Church friends who purchase cards often recruit others from their small groups, Sunday school classes, and ministry teams, creating natural expansion opportunities.

Idea 3: The Workplace Connection Strategy

"Faith in the Marketplace"

The Approach: Share Scripture cards with Christian coworkers and faith-friendly colleagues as encouragement gifts and stress-relief tools for the workplace environment.

Why It Works: The workplace creates natural opportunities for encouragement and gift-giving (birthdays, promotions, difficult seasons). Christians appreciate having faith-based tools that are professional yet meaningful.

"Team Success" Application: Workplace customers often invite you to share with their departments, leading to corporate chaplain opportunities and bulk sales to entire companies.

Idea 4: The Neighborhood Ambassador Approach

"Becoming the Community Encourager"

The Approach: Position yourself as the neighborhood's source of encouragement and spiritual support by offering Scripture cards for various life situations (new babies, illnesses, celebrations, challenges).

Why It Works: Neighbors appreciate practical expressions of care during life events. Scripture cards provide a non-threatening way to offer spiritual support while building meaningful community relationships.

"Team Success" Application: Successful neighborhood relationships often lead to opportunities in local schools, community organizations, and referrals to other neighborhoods.

Idea 5: The Social Media Friends Circle

"Digital Discipleship Through Cards"

The Approach: Share Scripture cards through your personal social media networks, focusing on encouraging friends during difficult seasons and celebrating victories with faith-based gifts.

Why It Works: Social media creates opportunities to minister to friends across geographic boundaries. Posts about Scripture cards naturally generate interest from people seeking encouragement and spiritual growth tools.

"Team Success" Application: Social media success often attracts other entrepreneurs who want to join your Mutual Success Team or start their own card ministry.

Idea 6: The Holiday Gift Strategy

"Sacred Seasons, Sacred Gifts"

The Approach: Position Scripture cards as meaningful alternatives to generic holiday gifts, especially for Christmas, Easter, graduations, and other spiritually significant occasions.

Why It Works: People struggle to find meaningful gifts that reflect their faith values. Scripture cards solve this problem while providing recipients with lasting spiritual value beyond the holiday moment.

"Team Success" Application: Holiday success creates year-round customers who return for birthdays, anniversaries, and other special occasions throughout the year.

Idea 7: The Birthday Blessing System

"Celebrating Life with Scripture"

The Approach: Create a systematic approach to giving Scripture cards as birthday gifts throughout the year, tracking friends' and family members' birthdays and preparing personalized card selections.

Why It Works: Birthdays occur year-round, creating consistent monthly sales opportunities. Personalized Scripture selections show thoughtfulness and create emotional connections that lead to referrals.

"Team Success" Application: Birthday gift recipients often ask where to purchase cards for their own gift-giving, creating new customer relationships and potential team members.

Idea 8: The Sympathy and Comfort Ministry

"Healing Hearts Through Scripture"

The Approach: Offer Scripture cards as comfort gifts during times of loss, illness, job challenges, and other difficult life circumstances, positioning yourself as a source of spiritual encouragement.

Why It Works: People experiencing difficulty are especially receptive to spiritual comfort. Scripture cards provide tangible hope that recipients can hold, read repeatedly, and treasure during healing processes.

"Team Success" Application: Comfort ministry often leads to opportunities in hospitals, nursing homes, and grief support groups, creating institutional sales relationships.

Idea 9: The Congratulations Package

"Celebrating Victories with Faith"

The Approach: Create celebration packages using Scripture cards to honor achievements, promotions, graduations, new babies, and other joyful life events in your network.

Why It Works: Celebration moments create positive emotional associations with your cards. Recipients associate your gifts with their happiest memories and share the experience with others.

"Team Success" Application: Celebration customers often request bulk packages for their own gift-giving needs, creating larger sales and potential business partnerships.

Idea 10: The Thank You Token Strategy

"Gratitude That Multiplies"

The Approach: Use Scripture cards as thank you gifts for people who provide favors, assistance, referrals, or kindness, creating a systematic appreciation ministry.

Why It Works: Thank you gifts are unexpected and create positive surprises that recipients remember. Scripture cards add spiritual significance to expressions of gratitude.

"Team Success" Application: Thank you recipients often become interested in purchasing cards for their own appreciation needs, creating reciprocal business relationships.

Idea 11: The Encouragement Subscription

"Monthly Blessings for Special People"

The Approach: Create monthly subscription arrangements where you provide different Scripture cards each month to people going through extended challenges or pursuing long-term goals.

Why It Works: Monthly touchpoints create ongoing relationships and recurring revenue. Recipients look forward to their monthly encouragement and often share their cards with others.

"Team Success" Application: Subscription customers often refer others who need ongoing encouragement, creating multiple recurring revenue streams.

Idea 12: The Small Group Integration

"Community Within Community"

The Approach: Partner with small group leaders to incorporate Scripture cards into group studies, prayer times, and member encouragement, creating group purchasing arrangements.

Why It Works: Small groups prioritize spiritual growth and member care. Scripture cards enhance both purposes while creating bulk sales opportunities.

"Team Success" Application: Successful small group partnerships often lead to opportunities with other groups and larger church partnerships.

Idea 13: The Teacher and Education Network

"Blessing Those Who Shape Minds"

The Approach: Connect with teachers, principals, and education professionals who appreciate faith-based encouragement tools for their stressful but meaningful work.

Why It Works: Educators face unique challenges and appreciate recognition for their service. Christian teachers especially value faith-based gifts that acknowledge their calling.

"Team Success" Application: Education networks create opportunities for school partnerships, classroom supplies sales, and connections with parent organizations.

Idea 14: The Healthcare Heroes Strategy

"Healing Hearts of Healers"

The Approach: Focus on nurses, doctors, therapists, and other healthcare workers who appreciate spiritual encouragement tools for their demanding and emotionally challenging careers.

Why It Works: Healthcare workers experience high stress and emotional burnout. Scripture cards provide spiritual refreshment and remind them of their calling to serve others.

"Team Success" Application: Healthcare relationships often lead to opportunities in hospitals, clinics, and medical professional organizations.

Idea 15: The Senior Saints Strategy

"Honoring Wisdom with Words"

The Approach: Connect with senior adults who appreciate tangible spiritual materials and often have more disposable income and gift-giving opportunities than younger demographics.

Why It Works: Seniors value tangible spiritual items they can hold and read. They often purchase cards for grandchildren, church friends, and community members they want to encourage.

"Team Success" Application: Senior customers often introduce you to their extensive church and community networks, creating multiple generational marketing opportunities.

Idea 16: The Parent Network Connection

"Connecting Hearts Through Children"

The Approach: Build relationships with other parents through school events, sports activities, and community programs, offering Scripture cards as family blessing tools.

Why It Works: Parents understand the challenge of instilling values in children. Scripture cards provide practical tools for family devotions and gift-giving to other families.

"Team Success" Application: Parent networks create opportunities for school fundraisers, team celebrations, and community family events.

Idea 17: The Men's Ministry Connection

"Strengthening Brothers in Faith"

The Approach: Partner with men's ministry leaders to provide Scripture cards for men's events, accountability groups, and workplace evangelism tools.

Why It Works: Men appreciate practical tools they can use in witnessing and encouragement. Scripture cards provide non-threatening ways for men to share faith in masculine environments.

"Team Success" Application: Men's ministry connections often lead to workplace opportunities and connections with other men's organizations.

Idea 18: The Women's Ministry Network

"Empowering Sisters in Service"

The Approach: Connect with women's ministry leaders to provide Scripture cards for retreats, Bible studies, and community outreach programs.

Why It Works: Women's ministries emphasize relationships, encouragement, and practical spiritual tools. Scripture cards align perfectly with women's ministry values and activities.

"Team Success" Application: Women's ministry success often creates opportunities with multiple churches and women's organizations across denominational lines.

Idea 19: The Young Professional Strategy

"Faith for the Future"

The Approach: Connect with young professionals who are building careers while maintaining faith commitments, offering Scripture cards as workplace encouragement and networking tools.

Why It Works: Young professionals face unique pressures balancing career ambitions with faith values. Scripture cards provide portable spiritual support for workplace challenges.

"Team Success" Application: Young professional networks often lead to corporate partnerships and opportunities with professional Christian organizations.

Idea 20: The Community Volunteer Connection

"Serving Together, Succeeding Together"

The Approach: Build relationships with fellow volunteers in community organizations, offering Scripture cards as appreciation gifts and tools for encouraging other volunteers.

Why It Works: Volunteers are service-oriented and appreciate tools that help them encourage others. Community involvement creates natural opportunities for gift-giving and relationship building.

"Team Success" Application: Volunteer networks often connect you with diverse community organizations and create opportunities for civic partnerships.

SECTION A SUMMARY: PERSONAL NETWORK FOUNDATIONS

These first 20 methods establish the foundation principle: **Team Success begins with existing relationships**. Every person in your current network represents an opportunity to:

- **Practice your presentation** in safe, supportive environments
- **Generate initial sales** that build confidence and momentum
- **Identify potential team members** who share your vision
- **Create referrals** to new networks and opportunities
- **Build testimonials** that validate your approach

The progression moves from closest relationships (family) to broader community connections, creating expanding circles of influence that naturally lead to the more advanced methods in subsequent sections.

Key Insight: Personal network success creates the credibility and confidence needed for the more challenging and profitable methods that follow. If you are able to try and master these 20 approaches first, then you'll have a solid foundation for unlimited "Team Success" expansions in the future. It's a possibility. But there are more options you can start with next also.

SECTION B: CHURCH AND MINISTRY PARTNERSHIPS

Transforming Congregations into Mutual Success Communities

Idea 21: The Sunday School Fundraiser Revolution

"From Bake Sales to Biblical Sales"

The Approach: Partner with Sunday school classes to replace traditional fundraising with Scripture card sales that both generate funds and advance spiritual growth simultaneously.

Why It Works: Sunday school classes constantly need funds for activities, missions, and projects. Scripture card sales create sustainable income while reinforcing class spiritual objectives and involving every member in meaningful ministry.

"Team Success" Application: Successful classes often recruit other classes, creating church-wide fundraising movements and establishing you as the go-to resource for ministry funding solutions.

Idea 22: The Youth Group Mission Trip Engine

"Funding Dreams Through Faith Cards"

The Approach: Help youth groups fund mission trips, camps, and activities by selling Scripture cards that connect with their evangelistic mission and provide practical fundraising results.

Why It Works: Youth groups struggle with expensive mission trips and limited fundraising options. Scripture card sales teach entrepreneurship while funding their ministry dreams and providing witnessing tools.

"Team Success" Application: Youth group success creates opportunities with youth camps, conferences, and denominational youth organizations across multiple states.

Idea 23: The Women's Ministry Boutique

"More Than Shopping, It's Ministry"

The Approach: Establish monthly women's ministry events featuring Scripture cards alongside other faith-based products, creating regular community-building and income opportunities.

Why It Works: Women's ministry events combine fellowship, spiritual growth, and practical shopping. Scripture cards appeal to women's gift-giving nature and desire for meaningful spiritual tools.

"Team Success" Application: Women's boutique success often leads to regional women's conferences and multi-church women's ministry partnerships.

Idea 24: The Men's Ministry Challenge

"Iron Sharpening Iron Through Sales"

The Approach: Create competitive challenges within men's ministry where teams compete to reach sales goals while using cards for workplace evangelism and family devotions.

Why It Works: Men respond to competition and challenges. Scripture card sales provide practical tools for workplace witnessing while creating brotherhood through shared goals and mutual accountability.

"Team Success" Application: Men's ministry success creates opportunities with other men's organizations, workplace chaplain programs, and business networking groups.

Idea 25: The VBS Marketplace Ministry

"Teaching Children Kingdom Economics"

The Approach: Integrate Scripture card sales into Vacation Bible School programming, teaching children entrepreneurship while providing parents with meaningful VBS takeaways.

Why It Works: VBS programs seek innovative ways to teach biblical principles. Scripture card sales demonstrate stewardship, work ethic, and evangelism while creating lasting family memories.

"Team Success" Application: VBS success creates opportunities with children's ministry conferences and summer camp programs across multiple denominations.

Idea 26: The Church Fair Partnership

"Community Events, Kingdom Impact"

The Approach: Partner with church fairs, festivals, and community outreach events to provide Scripture cards as both vendor products and ministry tools for visitor engagement.

Why It Works: Church fairs attract diverse community members seeking meaningful connections. Scripture cards provide natural conversation starters and tangible spiritual takeaways from church events.

"Team Success" Application: Church fair success creates relationships with event planners and opportunities for regional festival circuits.

Idea 27: The Pastor Appreciation Strategy

"Honoring Shepherds with Scripture"

The Approach: Create special pastor appreciation packages using Scripture cards focused on leadership, encouragement, and pastoral care, marketing to congregations during Pastor Appreciation Month.

Why It Works: Congregations want meaningful ways to honor their pastors beyond generic gifts. Scripture cards focused on pastoral themes show thoughtfulness while providing ongoing spiritual encouragement.

"Team Success" Application: Pastor appreciation success creates relationships with church leadership and opportunities for congregation-wide programs.

Idea 28: The Ministry Leader Network

"Equipping Leaders to Lead"

The Approach: Connect with ministry leaders across multiple churches and denominations, providing Scripture cards as leadership development tools and ministry resource alternatives.

Why It Works: Ministry leaders constantly seek fresh resources for leadership development and team building. Scripture cards provide portable, practical tools for leadership training and ministry team encouragement.

"Team Success" Application: Ministry leader networks create opportunities for leadership conferences, seminary partnerships, and denominational resource distribution.

Idea 29: The Retreat Center Partnership

"Sacred Spaces, Sacred Sales"

The Approach: Establish ongoing partnerships with Christian retreat centers, camps, and conference facilities to provide Scripture cards for all guests and program participants.

Why It Works: Retreat centers seek meaningful takeaways for guests that reinforce spiritual experiences. Scripture cards provide lasting reminders of retreat insights and spiritual breakthroughs.

"Team Success" Application: Retreat center success creates opportunities with retreat speakers, conference organizers, and national retreat networks.

Idea 30: The Denominational Conference Circuit

"Reaching Networks Through Networks"

The Approach: Establish vendor relationships with denominational conferences, conventions, and assemblies, positioning Scripture cards as universal tools that transcend denominational differences.

Why It Works: Denominational conferences attract motivated believers seeking spiritual growth tools. Scripture cards appeal across denominational lines while providing networking opportunities with church leaders.

"Team Success" Application: Conference success creates opportunities with national denominational leadership and multi-state church networks.

Idea 31: The Small Group Supply System

"Fueling Fellowship with Faith Cards"

The Approach: Create systematic supply relationships with small group leaders, providing different Scripture card themes for various study topics and group needs throughout the year.

Why It Works: Small groups need fresh resources for prayer, encouragement, and member care. Scripture cards provide flexible tools that enhance any study topic while building group unity.

"Team Success" Application: Small group success creates opportunities for church-wide small group ministries and inter-church small group networks.

Idea 32: The Missions Team Support

"Equipping Global Workers with Local Sales"

The Approach: Partner with missions teams to sell Scripture cards as pre-trip fundraising while providing cards as ministry tools for international outreach and cross-cultural ministry.

Why It Works: Missions teams need both funding and practical ministry tools. Scripture cards serve dual purposes while creating ongoing support relationships with missions-minded congregations.

"Team Success" Application: Missions success creates opportunities with missions agencies, international ministries, and global church planting organizations.

Idea 33: The Church Plant Partnership

"Growing New Churches Through Scripture Sales"

The Approach: Support church plants by establishing Scripture card sales teams that both fund church operations and create community connections for the new congregation.

Why It Works: Church plants need innovative funding sources and community outreach strategies. Scripture card sales provide both while building congregational unity around shared mission.

"Team Success" Application: Church plant success creates relationships with church planting networks and opportunities for multi-city expansion.

Idea 34: The Worship Team Ministry

"Harmonizing Hearts Through Scripture"

The Approach: Partner with worship teams to use Scripture cards for devotional preparation, audience engagement, and special music ministry enhancements.

Why It Works: Worship teams seek tools that enhance spiritual preparation and audience connection. Scripture cards provide practical devotional resources while creating unique ministry opportunities.

"Team Success" Application: Worship team success creates opportunities with music ministries, Christian concerts, and worship conferences.

Idea 35: The Children's Ministry Integration

"Teaching Tomorrow's Leaders Today"

The Approach: Work with children's ministry leaders to incorporate Scripture cards into Sunday school lessons, children's church programs, and family ministry initiatives.

Why It Works: Children's ministries need engaging tools that involve families and reinforce biblical lessons. Scripture cards provide tangible takeaways that continue ministry impact at home.

"Team Success" Application: Children's ministry success creates opportunities with Christian schools, daycare centers, and family ministry organizations.

Idea 36: The Senior Adult Ministry

"Honoring Wisdom, Sharing Scripture"

The Approach: Develop specialized Scripture card programs for senior adult ministries, focusing on legacy themes, grandparent resources, and intergenerational blessing tools.

Why It Works: Senior adults appreciate tangible spiritual resources and have established gift-giving patterns. Scripture cards provide meaningful tools for blessing grandchildren and sharing wisdom.

"Team Success" Application: Senior ministry success creates opportunities with retirement communities, nursing homes, and senior service organizations.

Idea 37: The College Ministry Connection

"Faith for the Future Generation"

The Approach: Partner with college ministries to provide Scripture cards as encouragement tools for students facing academic, financial, and life direction challenges.

Why It Works: College students experience unique pressures and appreciate practical spiritual support tools. Scripture cards provide affordable encouragement that fits student budgets and lifestyles.

"Team Success" Application: College ministry success creates opportunities with campus ministries nationwide and connections with young adult church plants.

Idea 38: The Prison Ministry Outreach

"Hope Behind Bars Through Scripture"

The Approach: Partner with prison ministries to provide Scripture cards as encouragement tools for inmates, family support resources, and volunteer appreciation gifts.

Why It Works: Prison ministries need practical tools that provide hope and spiritual growth resources for challenging environments. Scripture cards offer tangible encouragement that inmates can keep and treasure.

"Team Success" Application: Prison ministry success creates opportunities with correctional chaplains, reentry programs, and criminal justice reform organizations.

Idea 39: The Military Ministry Support

"Serving Those Who Serve"

The Approach: Connect with military ministries and chaplains to provide Scripture cards as deployment encouragement, family support tools, and veteran ministry resources.

Why It Works: Military families face unique challenges including deployments, relocations, and service-related stress. Scripture cards provide portable spiritual support that travels with military lifestyles.

"Team Success" Application: Military ministry success creates opportunities with base chaplains, veteran organizations, and military family support networks.

Idea 40: The Hospital Chaplain Partnership

"Healing Hearts in Healthcare Settings"

The Approach: Establish relationships with hospital chaplains and healthcare ministry programs to provide Scripture cards for patient encouragement, family support, and staff appreciation.

Why It Works: Healthcare settings create opportunities for spiritual ministry and encouragement. Scripture cards provide appropriate spiritual support that respects diverse beliefs while offering hope and comfort.

"Team Success" Application: Hospital chaplain success creates opportunities with healthcare systems, medical professional organizations, and patient advocacy groups.

SECTION B SUMMARY: CHURCH AND MINISTRY PARTNERSHIPS

Methods 21-40 demonstrate how **Team Success expands through institutional relationships**. These approaches create:

- **Systematic income streams** through organizational partnerships
- **Leadership credibility** through ministry leader endorsements
- **Network multiplication** through institutional connections
- **Ministry impact** that extends far beyond sales
- **Sustainable growth** through repeated program cycles

Key Insight: Ministry partnerships transform individual sales efforts into community movements. These relationships provide the foundation for the larger community impact methods that follow in Section C.

SECTION C: EVENTS AND SEASONAL STRATEGIES

Maximizing Team Success Through Community Engagement and Timing

Idea 41: The Craft Fair Circuit Mastery

"Artisan Markets, Kingdom Impact"

The Approach: Establish a regular presence at craft fairs and artisan markets, positioning Scripture cards as unique handcrafted spiritual gifts that stand out among typical craft items.

Why It Works: Craft fair attendees seek unique, meaningful items they can't find elsewhere. Scripture cards appeal to spiritual shoppers while offering practical gifts that support local artisans and ministry.

"Team Success" Application: Craft fair success creates opportunities for vendor team partnerships, regional craft circuits, and artisan cooperative relationships that multiply market presence.

Idea 42: The Christian Music Festival Network

"Concerts That Change Lives and Income"

The Approach: Establish vendor relationships with Christian music festivals, concerts, and outdoor events where spiritual audiences gather for entertainment and worship experiences.

Why It Works: Music festival attendees are spiritually engaged and seeking meaningful merchandise that extends their worship experience. Scripture cards provide lasting spiritual impact beyond the concert moment.

"Team Success" Application: Music festival success creates relationships with artists, promoters, and venue owners, leading to national tour opportunities and artist endorsements.

Idea 43: The Homeschool Convention Strategy

"Education Events, Eternal Impact"

The Approach: Target homeschool conventions and educational events where Christian families gather seeking curriculum, resources, and tools for faith-based education.

Why It Works: Homeschool families prioritize faith integration and seek educational tools that reinforce biblical values. Scripture cards provide perfect family devotion and character development resources.

"Team Success" Application: Homeschool success creates opportunities with curriculum publishers, co-op groups, and online homeschool communities across multiple states.

Idea 44: The Business Networking Breakthrough

"Professional Connections, Kingdom Conversations"

The Approach: Attend Christian business networking events, chambers of commerce, and professional meetups, using Scripture cards as unique business gifts and conversation starters.

Why It Works: Christian business professionals seek ways to integrate faith with work and appreciate tools that facilitate workplace witnessing and client encouragement.

"Team Success" Application: Business networking creates opportunities for corporate partnerships, executive gift programs, and professional referral networks.

Idea 45: The Farmers Market Ministry

"Fresh Produce, Fresh Purpose"

The Approach: Establish weekly presence at farmers markets where community members gather for local shopping and social interaction, offering Scripture cards as community blessing tools.

Why It Works: Farmers markets attract people seeking authentic, locally-sourced products. Scripture cards fit this desire for meaningful, personal items while creating weekly community presence.

"Team Success" Application: Farmers market success creates relationships with other vendors, market organizers, and opportunities for seasonal festival participation.

Idea 46: The Wedding Show Partnership

"Sacred Ceremonies, Sacred Gifts"

The Approach: Participate in bridal expos and wedding shows, positioning Scripture cards as unique wedding favors, anniversary gifts, and marriage blessing tools.

Why It Works: Wedding planning involves extensive gift-giving needs and desire for meaningful ceremony elements. Scripture cards provide spiritual significance for sacred ceremonies and celebrations.

"Team Success" Application: Wedding success creates relationships with wedding planners, venues, and opportunities for anniversary and family celebration markets.

Idea 47: The Graduation Gift Campaign

"Celebrating Achievement with Scripture"

The Approach: Create seasonal campaigns targeting graduation celebrations from elementary through college levels, positioning Scripture cards as meaningful achievement recognition gifts.

Why It Works: Graduation seasons create concentrated gift-giving opportunities. Scripture cards provide spiritual significance for achievement celebrations while offering practical encouragement for life transitions.

"Team Success" Application: Graduation success creates opportunities with schools, colleges, and educational institutions for systematic celebration programs.

Idea 48: The Back-to-School Special

"New Seasons, New Encouragement"

The Approach: Develop back-to-school campaigns targeting teachers, students, and parents with Scripture cards designed for educational encouragement and classroom blessing.

Why It Works: Back-to-school seasons create natural opportunities for encouragement gifts and educational resource purchases. Scripture cards provide spiritual support for academic challenges and achievements.

"Team Success" Application: Back-to-school success creates relationships with educators, school systems, and parent organizations for ongoing educational partnerships.

Idea 49: The Mother's Day Ministry

"Honoring Mothers with Scripture"

The Approach: Create Mother's Day campaigns in churches and communities, positioning Scripture cards as meaningful alternatives to traditional flowers and generic gifts.

Why It Works: Mother's Day creates universal gift-giving opportunities with emphasis on meaningful, lasting presents. Scripture cards provide spiritual significance that mothers treasure beyond the holiday.

"Team Success" Application: Mother's Day success creates opportunities with florists, gift shops, and ongoing family celebration markets throughout the year.

Idea 50: The Father's Day Focus

"Strengthening Fathers with Scripture"

The Approach: Develop Father's Day programs targeting dads with Scripture cards focused on fatherhood, leadership, and family strength themes.

Why It Works: Father's Day often lacks meaningful gift options for spiritual men. Scripture cards provide practical tools for family leadership and spiritual growth that fathers actually use.

"Team Success" Application: Father's Day success creates opportunities with men's organizations, father-focused ministries, and family service organizations.

Idea 51: The Valentine's Ministry

"Love Letters from Heaven"

The Approach: Position Scripture cards as unique Valentine's gifts that express both romantic love and spiritual blessing, targeting couples seeking meaningful relationship tools.

Why It Works: Valentine's Day emphasizes love and meaningful expressions. Scripture cards provide spiritual depth to romantic celebrations while offering practical marriage strengthening tools.

"Team Success" Application: Valentine's success creates opportunities with marriage ministries, counselors, and ongoing relationship enrichment markets.

Idea 52: The Easter Celebration Strategy

"Resurrection Hope, Renewed Purpose"

The Approach: Create Easter campaigns focusing on resurrection themes, new life, and spiritual renewal, positioning Scripture cards as meaningful Easter gifts and church outreach tools.

Why It Works: Easter creates opportunities for spiritual gift-giving and church outreach. Scripture cards provide lasting spiritual impact beyond Easter candy and decorations.

"Team Success" Application: Easter success creates opportunities with churches for seasonal outreach programs and year-round evangelism tool partnerships.

Idea 53: The Christmas Market Mastery

"Sacred Season, Sacred Gifts"

The Approach: Establish comprehensive Christmas market presence at holiday events, positioning Scripture cards as meaningful alternatives to commercial Christmas gifts.

Why It Works: Christmas creates maximum gift-giving opportunities with emphasis on spiritual significance. Scripture cards provide lasting spiritual value beyond temporary holiday items.

"Team Success" Application: Christmas success creates year-round customer relationships and opportunities for seasonal vendor partnerships and holiday market circuits.

Idea 54: The Thanksgiving Gratitude Campaign

"Grateful Hearts, Grateful Gifts"

The Approach: Develop Thanksgiving campaigns focusing on gratitude themes, family blessing, and appreciation gifts using Scripture cards that emphasize thankfulness and God's provision.

Why It Works: Thanksgiving emphasizes gratitude and family connection. Scripture cards provide meaningful tools for expressing thanksgiving and creating family devotion opportunities.

"Team Success" Application: Thanksgiving success creates opportunities with family service organizations and seasonal gratitude-focused community programs.

Idea 55: The New Year Resolution Support

"Fresh Starts, Fresh Scripture"

The Approach: Create New Year campaigns targeting people making spiritual resolutions and seeking encouragement tools for personal growth and life change goals.

Why It Works: New Year creates motivation for spiritual growth and personal improvement. Scripture cards provide daily encouragement tools that support resolution success and spiritual development.

"Team Success" Application: New Year success creates opportunities with fitness centers, counseling services, and personal development organizations.

Idea 56: The Summer Camp Partnership

"Camp Memories, Eternal Impact"

The Approach: Establish partnerships with Christian summer camps, providing Scripture cards for camper encouragement, counselor training, and parent communication programs.

Why It Works: Summer camps create intensive spiritual growth environments where Scripture cards enhance devotional times, provide comfort during homesickness, and create lasting camp memories.

"Team Success" Application: Summer camp success creates opportunities with camp networks, outdoor ministries, and year-round youth program partnerships.

Idea 57: The Community Festival Circuit

"Celebrating Community, Sharing Scripture"

The Approach: Establish regular participation in community festivals, county fairs, and civic celebrations, using Scripture cards to create positive Christian presence in secular events.

Why It Works: Community festivals attract diverse audiences seeking entertainment and unique vendors. Scripture cards provide non-threatening Christian witness while offering practical community blessing tools.

"Team Success" Application: Festival success creates relationships with event organizers, civic leaders, and opportunities for year-round community involvement and partnerships.

Idea 58: The Holiday Bazaar Network

"Bazaars That Bless and Build"

The Approach: Participate in church and community holiday bazaars, positioning Scripture cards among traditional craft items while creating unique spiritual shopping experiences.

Why It Works: Holiday bazaars combine shopping with community fellowship. Scripture cards provide meaningful alternatives to typical bazaar items while supporting event fundraising goals.

"Team Success" Application: Bazaar success creates relationships with church event organizers and opportunities for multi-church bazaar participation and seasonal vendor networks.

Idea 59: The Health Fair Ministry

"Healing Bodies, Encouraging Souls"

The Approach: Participate in health fairs and wellness events, positioning Scripture cards as emotional and spiritual wellness tools that complement physical health initiatives.

Why It Works: Health fairs attract people seeking holistic wellness solutions. Scripture cards provide spiritual and emotional health resources that address complete personal wellness needs.

"Team Success" Application: Health fair success creates opportunities with healthcare providers, wellness centers, and medical professional partnerships.

Idea 60: The Sports Tournament Ministry

"Competition and Character Building"

The Approach: Partner with Christian sports leagues and tournaments, providing Scripture cards for team encouragement, character development, and sportsmanship recognition programs.

Why It Works: Sports environments create opportunities for character development and team building. Scripture cards provide practical tools for coaches to reinforce spiritual principles through athletic participation.

"Team Success" Application: Sports tournament success creates opportunities with athletic departments, coaching associations, and youth sports organization partnerships.

SECTION C SUMMARY: EVENTS AND SEASONAL STRATEGIES

Methods 41-60 demonstrate how **Team Success multiplies through strategic timing and community engagement**. These approaches create:

- **Seasonal revenue spikes** that boost annual income significantly
- **Community visibility** that establishes local market presence
- **Network expansion** through vendor relationships and event connections
- **Market diversification** beyond church and ministry boundaries
- **Brand recognition** that builds long-term customer loyalty

Key Insight: Event and seasonal strategies transform Team Success from relationship-dependent to market-driven, creating systematic income opportunities that repeat annually while building broader community influence and customer base expansion.

SECTION D: DIGITAL AND ADVANCED STRATEGIES

Leveraging Technology and Innovation for Exponential Team Success

Idea 61: The Facebook Marketplace Mastery

"Local Digital, Global Impact"

The Approach: Establish systematic presence on Facebook Marketplace, targeting local Christian communities with Scripture cards positioned as meaningful gifts and spiritual encouragement tools.

Why It Works: Facebook Marketplace combines local trust with digital convenience. Christian buyers appreciate faith-based sellers they can research through profiles, creating confidence in both product and seller integrity.

"Team Success" Application: Facebook success creates opportunities for social media team partnerships, digital marketing collaborations, and online customer community building.

Idea 62: The Instagram Stories Strategy

"Visual Storytelling for Scripture Sales"

The Approach: Use Instagram Stories to showcase Scripture cards through daily encouragement posts, customer testimonials, and behind-the-scenes business content that builds authentic connections.

Why It Works: Instagram Stories create intimate, authentic connections with followers. Visual Scripture presentations appeal to spiritual audiences seeking daily inspiration and meaningful content.

"Team Success" Application: Instagram success attracts other content creators for collaboration opportunities and influencer partnership programs.

Idea 63: The YouTube Ministry Channel

"Content Creation That Converts"

The Approach: Create YouTube content featuring Scripture card unboxings, devotional readings, and customer testimonies that demonstrate product value while building ministry platform.

Why It Works: YouTube provides unlimited reach for spiritual content. Video demonstrations allow customers to experience Scripture cards virtually before purchasing, increasing conversion rates and customer satisfaction.

"Team Success" Application: YouTube success creates opportunities for Christian content creator networks, sponsorship deals, and national ministry platform development.

Idea 64: The Pinterest Inspiration Boards

"Visual Discovery for Scripture Gifts"

The Approach: Create Pinterest boards showcasing Scripture cards in various gift-giving scenarios, holiday displays, and spiritual practice settings to inspire purchase decisions.

Why It Works: Pinterest users actively seek gift ideas and spiritual inspiration. Visual presentations of Scripture cards in lifestyle contexts help customers envision practical applications and purchase scenarios.

"Team Success" Application: Pinterest success creates opportunities for lifestyle brand partnerships, home décor collaborations, and gift industry connections.

Idea 65: The TikTok Scripture Moments

"Micro-Ministry for Maximum Impact"

The Approach: Create short-form TikTok content featuring daily Scripture card readings, encouragement messages, and creative ways to use cards for spiritual growth.

Why It Works: TikTok reaches younger Christian audiences seeking authentic spiritual content. Short, engaging videos showcase Scripture cards' versatility while building ministry influence with next generation believers.

"Team Success" Application: TikTok success creates opportunities for youth ministry partnerships, young adult conferences, and Gen Z Christian influencer networks.

Idea 66: The Email Newsletter Empire

"Consistent Communication, Consistent Sales"

The Approach: Build email subscriber lists through free Scripture card samples and weekly encouragement newsletters that feature new products, customer stories, and spiritual content.

Why It Works: Email newsletters create direct customer communication channels. Regular spiritual content builds trust and positions Scripture cards as essential tools for ongoing spiritual growth.

"Team Success" Application: Email success creates opportunities for newsletter partnerships, content collaborations, and subscriber list sharing with complementary ministries.

Idea 67: The Blog Ministry Platform

"Written Words That Win Hearts"

The Approach: Create blog content featuring Scripture card devotionals, customer testimonies, and spiritual growth articles that naturally integrate product recommendations and purchase opportunities.

Why It Works: Blog content provides long-term SEO value and establishes thought leadership in Christian living. Educational content builds trust while demonstrating Scripture card applications in daily spiritual practice.

"Team Success" Application: Blog success creates opportunities for guest posting, ministry partnerships, and book publishing deals that expand platform influence.

Idea 68: The Online Christian Forums

"Community Participation for Ministry Growth"

The Approach: Participate authentically in online Christian communities and forums, offering Scripture cards as helpful resources for spiritual questions and community needs.

Why It Works: Forum participation builds genuine relationships and establishes expertise in Christian living. Natural product recommendations within helpful responses create authentic sales opportunities.

"Team Success" Application: Forum success creates opportunities for community moderator roles, online ministry partnerships, and digital discipleship programs.

Idea 69: The Zoom Party Sales

"Virtual Gatherings, Real Relationships"

The Approach: Host virtual Scripture card parties through Zoom, combining social fellowship with product demonstrations and group purchase opportunities for geographically dispersed customers.

Why It Works: Virtual parties overcome geographic limitations while creating social purchase experiences. Group dynamics and peer recommendations increase individual purchase decisions and create community around products.

"Team Success" Application: Zoom success creates opportunities for virtual team training, online coaching programs, and digital ministry expansion across multiple time zones.

Idea 70: The Text Message Marketing

"Personal Communication, Personal Sales"

The Approach: Build text subscriber lists for sharing daily Scripture verses, special offers, and personal encouragement messages that maintain consistent customer contact and drive repeat sales.

Why It Works: Text messages create immediate, personal communication that customers read within minutes. Personal touches and timely encouragement build strong customer relationships and purchase loyalty.

"Team Success" Application: Text marketing success creates opportunities for automated systems, customer service improvements, and personalized ministry programs.

Idea 71: The Podcast Sponsorship Strategy

"Audio Influence for Scripture Sales"

The Approach: Sponsor Christian podcasts and radio shows, positioning Scripture cards as practical tools that enhance listeners' spiritual growth and daily devotional practices.

Why It Works: Podcast sponsorships reach targeted Christian audiences during intimate listening experiences. Host endorsements create trust and credibility that drives immediate purchase decisions.

"Team Success" Application: Podcast success creates opportunities for show partnerships, speaking engagements, and audio content creation that builds ministry platform.

Idea 72: The Webinar Workshop Series

"Education That Elevates and Sells"

The Approach: Host educational webinars teaching spiritual growth principles while demonstrating how Scripture cards enhance prayer, meditation, and daily devotional practices.

Why It Works: Educational webinars establish expertise while providing value to participants. Product demonstrations within educational context create natural purchase opportunities without aggressive sales pressure.

"Team Success" Application: Webinar success creates opportunities for online course development, coaching programs, and digital ministry expansion.

Idea 73: The Online Marketplace Domination

"E-commerce Excellence for Scripture Sales"

The Approach: Establish strong presence on multiple online marketplaces (Etsy, Amazon, eBay) with optimized listings, customer reviews, and strategic pricing for Scripture cards.

Why It Works: Online marketplaces provide built-in customer traffic and trust systems. Professional listings with positive reviews create credibility while marketplace algorithms promote high-performing products.

"Team Success" Application: Marketplace success creates opportunities for wholesale partnerships, international sales, and private label product development.

Idea 74: The Affiliate Marketing Network

"Recruiting Others to Sell for You"

The Approach: Create affiliate programs where other ministry leaders and content creators promote Scripture cards for commissions, expanding reach through trusted voices in Christian communities.

Why It Works: Affiliate marketing leverages other people's audiences and credibility. Commission-based partnerships align interests while expanding market reach beyond individual capacity.

"Team Success" Application: Affiliate success creates opportunities for network marketing programs, team leadership development, and passive income generation.

Idea 75: The Digital Product Bundle

"Adding Value Through Digital Resources"

The Approach: Create digital products (devotional guides, prayer journals, study materials) that complement physical Scripture cards, increasing average order value and customer satisfaction.

Why It Works: Digital bundles provide additional value while increasing profit margins. Complementary resources enhance Scripture card usage while creating premium product offerings for serious customers.

"Team Success" Application: Digital success creates opportunities for online course development, membership sites, and intellectual property licensing deals.

Idea 76: The Virtual Reality Scripture Experience

"Cutting-Edge Technology for Ancient Truth"

The Approach: Partner with technology companies to create virtual reality experiences that complement Scripture cards, positioning products at the intersection of innovation and spirituality.

Why It Works: VR technology creates immersive spiritual experiences that appeal to tech-savvy Christians. Innovative approaches demonstrate commitment to reaching modern audiences with timeless truth.

"Team Success" Application: VR success creates opportunities for technology partnerships, conference speaking, and positioning as innovation leader in Christian products.

Idea 77: The Mobile App Integration

"Smartphones for Scripture Success"

The Approach: Develop mobile apps that complement physical Scripture cards with digital features like audio readings, sharing capabilities, and progress tracking for spiritual growth goals.

Why It Works: Mobile apps extend product value while creating ongoing customer engagement. Digital features enhance physical product usage while building customer data and loyalty programs.

"Team Success" Application: App success creates opportunities for software partnerships, technology licensing, and digital ministry platform development.

Idea 78: The AI-Powered Personalization

"Artificial Intelligence for Personal Ministry"

The Approach: Use AI technology to create personalized Scripture card recommendations based on customer spiritual needs, life circumstances, and growth goals.

Why It Works: AI personalization creates unique customer experiences that demonstrate deep understanding of individual spiritual needs. Customized recommendations increase purchase satisfaction and customer loyalty.

"Team Success" Application: AI success creates opportunities for technology consulting, software licensing, and positioning as innovation leader in personalized ministry.

Idea 79: The Blockchain Scripture Registry

"Cryptocurrency Meets Christian Ministry"

The Approach: Create blockchain-based systems for tracking Scripture card impact, customer testimonies, and ministry outcomes, appealing to tech-forward Christian communities.

Why It Works: Blockchain technology appeals to innovative Christians interested in transparent, secure systems. Technology integration demonstrates commitment to accountability and verifiable ministry impact.

"Team Success" Application: Blockchain success creates opportunities for cryptocurrency partnerships, tech conference speaking, and positioning as ministry innovation leader.

Idea 80: The Metaverse Ministry Platform

"Virtual Worlds for Real Scripture Impact"

The Approach: Establish presence in virtual worlds and metaverse platforms, creating digital spaces where Scripture cards can be experienced and purchased in virtual environments.

Why It Works: Metaverse platforms reach digital native Christians comfortable with virtual interactions. Virtual presence demonstrates commitment to meeting people where they spend time online.

"Team Success" Application: Metaverse success creates opportunities for virtual real estate partnerships, digital ministry consulting, and next-generation platform development.

SECTION D SUMMARY: DIGITAL AND ADVANCED STRATEGIES

Methods 61-80 demonstrate how **Team Success leverages technology for exponential growth and market expansion**. These approaches create:

- **Scalable digital systems** that work beyond geographic limitations
- **Technology leadership** that positions you as ministry innovation pioneer
- **Automated income streams** that generate revenue while you sleep
- **Data-driven insights** that optimize all marketing and sales efforts
- **Competitive advantages** that separate you from traditional ministry approaches

Key Insight: Digital and advanced strategies transform Team Success from labor-intensive to system-dependent, creating sustainable business models that can scale globally while maintaining personal ministry impact and authentic relationship building.

SECTION E: ADVANCED AND CREATIVE STRATEGIES

Revolutionary Approaches for Extraordinary Team Success and Kingdom Impact

Idea 81: The Corporate Chaplain Network

"Bringing Scripture to the Workplace"

The Approach: Partner with corporate chaplains and workplace ministry organizations to provide Scripture cards as employee encouragement tools, stress management resources, and spiritual care supplies.

Why It Works: Corporate environments create unique opportunities for spiritual ministry and employee care. Scripture cards provide appropriate, non-denominational spiritual support that helps companies demonstrate care for employee well-being.

"Team Success" Application: Corporate success creates opportunities for business-to-business sales, employee assistance programs, and workplace ministry consulting services.

Idea 82: The Hospital Gift Shop Partnership

"Healing Environments, Hopeful Messages"

The Approach: Establish wholesale relationships with hospital gift shops, positioning Scripture cards as appropriate spiritual comfort items for patients, families, and medical staff.

"Hope Behind Bars, Freedom Through Scripture"

The Approach: Partner with correctional facilities and prison ministries to provide Scripture cards for inmate encouragement, family communication, and reentry preparation programs.

Why It Works: Prison environments create intense spiritual hunger and desire for hope. Scripture cards provide tangible spiritual resources that inmates can keep, study, and share with others.

"Team Success" Application: Prison ministry success creates opportunities with correctional chaplains, reentry organizations, and criminal justice reform initiatives.

Idea 85: The Military Base Outreach

"Serving Those Who Serve Our Country"

The Approach: Establish relationships with military base chaplains and family service organizations, providing Scripture cards for deployment care packages, family support, and veteran ministry.

Why It Works: Military service creates unique spiritual challenges including separation, danger, and transition stress. Scripture cards provide portable spiritual support that travels with military lifestyles.

"Team Success" Application: Military success creates opportunities with veteran organizations, defense contractors, and patriotic civic groups across multiple bases.

Idea 86: The College Campus Ministry

"Faith for the Future Generation"

The Approach: Partner with college campus ministries and student organizations, providing Scripture cards for student encouragement, exam stress relief, and spiritual growth programs.

Why It Works: College environments create intense academic and social pressures. Scripture cards provide practical spiritual support during stressful periods while building lifelong spiritual habits.

"Team Success" Application: Campus success creates opportunities with university systems, student affairs departments, and national college ministry organizations.

Idea 87: The Christian Business Network

"Faith-Based Commerce for Kingdom Growth"

The Approach: Establish exclusive partnerships with Christian business networks and chambers of commerce, positioning Scripture cards as premium client gifts and employee appreciation tools.

Why It Works: Christian business owners seek ways to integrate faith with commerce while demonstrating values to clients and employees. Scripture cards provide appropriate spiritual tools for business relationships.

"Team Success" Application: Business network success creates opportunities for corporate consulting, executive coaching, and commercial real estate partnerships.

Idea 88: The Real Estate Closing Gift Program

"Blessing New Beginnings with Scripture"

The Approach: Partner with Christian real estate agents to provide Scripture cards as unique closing gifts that bless new homeowners and create memorable transaction experiences.

Why It Works: Real estate transactions create emotional milestone moments where meaningful gifts are appreciated. Scripture cards provide spiritual significance for new home blessings and life transitions.

"Team Success" Application: Real estate success creates opportunities with mortgage companies, home builders, and property management organizations.

Idea 89: The Medical Office Partnership

"Healing Spaces, Encouraging Words"

The Approach: Establish relationships with Christian medical professionals, providing Scripture cards for patient encouragement, waiting room inspiration, and staff appreciation programs.

Why It Works: Medical environments create anxiety and stress where spiritual encouragement is welcomed. Scripture cards provide appropriate spiritual support that complements medical care.

"Team Success" Application: Medical success creates opportunities with healthcare networks, medical professional associations, and patient advocacy organizations.

Idea 90: The Subscription Box Empire

"Monthly Blessings, Recurring Revenue"

The Approach: Create subscription box services featuring curated Scripture cards with seasonal themes, special occasions, and spiritual growth focuses that deliver monthly spiritual encouragement.

Why It Works: Subscription models create predictable recurring revenue while providing ongoing customer value. Monthly spiritual content maintains engagement while building long-term customer relationships.

"Team Success" Application: Subscription success creates opportunities for product licensing, fulfillment partnerships, and subscription box network collaborations.

Idea 91: The Disaster Relief Ministry

"Hope in Crisis, Strength in Scripture"

The Approach: Establish rapid response partnerships with disaster relief organizations, providing Scripture cards for crisis comfort, volunteer encouragement, and community healing programs.

Why It Works: Disaster situations create intense spiritual needs where immediate encouragement is essential. Scripture cards provide portable spiritual support that disaster relief teams can easily distribute.

"Team Success" Application: Disaster relief success creates opportunities with emergency services, nonprofit organizations, and community resilience programs.

Idea 92: The Celebrity Endorsement Strategy

"Famous Voices for Faith-Based Products"

The Approach: Secure endorsements from Christian celebrities, athletes, and public figures who use Scripture cards for personal spiritual growth and public ministry.

Why It Works: Celebrity endorsements create instant credibility and market reach. Christian celebrities appreciate authentic spiritual tools they can genuinely recommend to their audiences.

"Team Success" Application: Celebrity success creates opportunities for entertainment industry partnerships, sports marketing deals, and media platform development.

Idea 93: The Government Chaplain Network

"Serving Public Servants with Scripture"

The Approach: Partner with government chaplains in military, police, fire, and civic services, providing Scripture cards for public servant encouragement and community service programs.

Why It Works: Public service creates high-stress environments where spiritual support is appreciated. Scripture cards provide appropriate spiritual resources that serve diverse public servant populations.

"Team Success" Application: Government success creates opportunities with civic organizations, public safety departments, and community service networks.

Idea 94: The Entertainment Industry Ministry

"Hollywood for Heaven's Kingdom"

The Approach: Establish relationships within the entertainment industry, providing Scripture cards for production crews, talent encouragement, and industry ministry programs.

Why It Works: Entertainment industry creates unique spiritual challenges where authentic faith resources are valued. Scripture cards provide practical spiritual support for high-pressure creative environments.

"Team Success" Application: Entertainment success creates opportunities for media partnerships, production company relationships, and celebrity ministry programs.

Idea 95: The Sports Team Ministry

"Character Building Through Competition"

The Approach: Partner with professional and amateur sports teams, providing Scripture cards for character development, team building, and fan ministry programs.

Why It Works: Sports environments create opportunities for character development and team unity. Scripture cards provide practical tools for coaches and chaplains to reinforce spiritual principles through athletic participation.

"Team Success" Application: Sports success creates opportunities with athletic departments, coaching associations, and sports ministry organizations nationwide.

Idea 96: The Theme Park Partnership

"Family Fun with Faith Foundation"

The Approach: Establish relationships with Christian theme parks and family entertainment venues, providing Scripture cards for visitor gifts, employee encouragement, and family ministry programs.

Why It Works: Family entertainment creates opportunities for wholesome ministry and family blessing. Scripture cards provide appropriate spiritual content that enhances family vacation experiences.

"Team Success" Application: Theme park success creates opportunities with tourism boards, family entertainment networks, and vacation ministry programs.

Idea 97: The Cruise Ship Ministry

"Sailing with Scripture, Ministering on Water"

The Approach: Partner with Christian cruise lines and ship chaplains, providing Scripture cards for passenger encouragement, crew ministry, and onboard spiritual programs.

Why It Works: Cruise environments create unique opportunities for spiritual ministry and personal reflection. Scripture cards provide portable spiritual resources perfect for vacation contemplation and ministry.

"Team Success" Application: Cruise success creates opportunities with travel ministries, vacation Bible programs, and international maritime ministry organizations.

Idea 98: The Space Program Ministry

"Infinite Space, Infinite Grace"

The Approach: Partner with space industry chaplains and aerospace organizations, providing Scripture cards for astronaut encouragement, mission blessing, and space industry ministry programs.

Why It Works: Space exploration creates profound spiritual questions about creation, purpose, and humanity's place in the universe. Scripture cards provide spiritual resources that address these cosmic contemplations.

"Team Success" Application: Space success creates opportunities for scientific ministry partnerships, STEM education programs, and creation science organizations.

SUMMARY: ADVANCED AND CREATIVE STRATEGIES

Methods 81-100 represent the **pinnacle of Team Success innovation and market expansion**. These approaches create:

- **Maximum market differentiation** through unique, hard-to-replicate partnerships
- **Premium pricing opportunities** due to specialized applications and limited competition
- **Media attention and publicity** through innovative and newsworthy partnerships
- **Institutional credibility** that opens doors to previously inaccessible markets
- **Legacy impact** that transforms communities and influences entire industries

Final Insight: Advanced and creative strategies transform Team Success from business opportunity to cultural movement, creating sustainable impact that extends far beyond individual income to community transformation, industry influence, and Kingdom advancement on a scale that fulfills the ultimate vision of "no need among them."

RETAIL REVOLUTION STRATEGY IDEAS

Transforming Commerce Through Scripture-Based Team Success

Idea 99: The Big Box Store Partnership

"Scripture in Secular Retail Environments"

The Approach: Establish wholesale relationships with major retail chains by positioning Scripture cards as spiritual wellness products that serve diverse customer spiritual needs in mainstream retail environments.

Why It Works: Big box retailers seek unique products that appeal to spiritual demographics while serving broad customer bases. Scripture cards provide appropriate spiritual content for diverse retail environments.

"Team Success" Application: Retail success creates opportunities with distribution networks, product placement services, and national retail partnerships.

Idea 100: The Specialty Store Network

"Curated Retail for Spiritual Consumers"

The Approach: Partner with specialty gift stores, boutiques, and curated retail environments to provide Scripture cards as premium spiritual gifts and meaningful merchandise.

Why It Works: Specialty retail seeks unique, meaningful products that justify premium pricing and create customer loyalty. Scripture cards provide spiritual significance that appeals to conscious consumers.

"Team Success" Application: Specialty success creates opportunities with gift industry, boutique networks, and premium retail partnerships.

Idea 101: The Online Marketplace Domination

"E-commerce Excellence for Scripture Distribution"

The Approach: Establish dominant presence across all major online marketplaces with optimized listings, strategic pricing, and comprehensive customer service for Scripture card sales.

Why It Works: Online marketplaces provide global reach with built-in customer trust and logistics systems. Professional marketplace presence creates credibility while algorithms promote high-performing products.

"Team Success" Application: E-commerce success creates opportunities for international sales, marketplace consulting, and digital distribution partnerships.

Idea 102: The Subscription Box Integration

"Monthly Spiritual Surprise Delivery"

The Approach: Partner with subscription box services and create dedicated spiritual subscription offerings featuring curated Scripture cards with seasonal themes and spiritual growth focuses.

Why It Works: Subscription models create predictable recurring revenue while providing ongoing customer value. Monthly spiritual content maintains engagement while building long-term customer relationships.

"Team Success" Application: Subscription success creates opportunities with fulfillment companies, product curation services, and recurring revenue partnerships.

Idea 103: The Pop-up Shop Strategy

"Temporary Retail for Maximum Impact"

The Approach: Create temporary retail experiences in high-traffic locations, seasonal markets, and event spaces to provide immersive Scripture card shopping experiences.

Why It Works: Pop-up retail creates urgency, novelty, and experiential shopping that appeals to modern consumers. Temporary installations allow testing new markets without long-term commitments.

"Team Success" Application: Pop-up success creates opportunities with event organizers, retail space providers, and experiential marketing companies.

Idea 104: The Corporate Gift Program

"B2B Scripture for Business Relationships"

The Approach: Develop corporate gift programs targeting businesses seeking meaningful client gifts, employee appreciation, and spiritual corporate social responsibility initiatives.

Why It Works: Corporate gifting requires meaningful, appropriate gifts that reflect company values. Scripture cards provide spiritual significance that demonstrates corporate character and values.

"Team Success" Application: Corporate success creates opportunities with business networks, gift industry, and corporate consulting services.

Idea 105: The Retail Training Institute

"Educating Retailers on Scripture Card Success"

The Approach: Create training programs for retailers on effectively selling Scripture cards, including customer education, display strategies, and spiritual product merchandising.

Why It Works: Retail training improves sales effectiveness while building retailer confidence and competence. Educational programs position you as industry expert while creating ongoing retailer relationships.

"Team Success" Application: Training success creates opportunities with retail associations, merchandising companies, and business education programs.

Idea 106: The Wholesale Distribution Network

"Systematic Scripture Distribution Excellence"

The Approach: Establish comprehensive wholesale distribution networks that serve retailers nationwide with efficient logistics, competitive pricing, and superior customer service.

Why It Works: Wholesale distribution creates scalable business models with predictable revenue streams. Professional distribution networks enable market expansion without individual retail relationship management.

"Team Success" Application: Distribution success creates opportunities with logistics companies, warehousing services, and national retail networks.

Idea 107: The Retail Technology Integration

"Digital Innovation for Physical Retail"

The Approach: Partner with retail technology companies to integrate Scripture cards with point-of-sale systems, inventory management, and customer relationship management for enhanced retail experiences.

Why It Works: Retail technology improves efficiency, customer experience, and sales tracking while providing competitive advantages. Technology integration demonstrates innovation leadership in spiritual products.

"Team Success" Application: Technology success creates opportunities with software companies, retail consultants, and innovation partnerships.

Idea 108: The International Retail Expansion

"Global Scripture Commerce Development"

The Approach: Develop international retail partnerships and distribution networks to bring Scripture cards to global markets through strategic international expansion.

Why It Works: International expansion multiplies market opportunities while serving global spiritual needs. Strategic international development creates sustainable global business growth.

"Team Success" Application: International success creates opportunities with global distributors, export services, and international business development.

Why It Works: Hospital environments create intense needs for spiritual comfort and encouragement. Scripture cards provide non-threatening spiritual support that respects diverse beliefs while offering hope during medical crises.

"Team Success" Application: Hospital success creates opportunities for healthcare system partnerships, medical professional organizations, and patient care program development.

Idea 83: The Nursing Home Ministry Program

"Dignity and Hope for Senior Living"

The Approach: Develop comprehensive programs for nursing homes and assisted living facilities, providing Scripture cards for resident encouragement, family communication, and staff appreciation.

Why It Works: Senior living environments create opportunities for meaningful spiritual ministry and intergenerational connection. Scripture cards provide tangible spiritual resources that residents can hold, read, and treasure.

"Team Success" Application: Nursing home success creates opportunities for senior care networks, family service organizations, and intergenerational ministry programs.

Idea 84: The Prison Ministry Transformation

GOVERNMENT AND MILITARY IDEAS

Serving Those Who Serve Through Scripture-Based Team Success

Idea 109: The Military Base Ministry Network

"Serving Those Who Serve Our Nation"

The Approach: Establish comprehensive partnerships with military base chaplains and family service organizations across all branches, providing Scripture cards for service member encouragement, family support, and deployment comfort.

Why It Works: Military service creates unique spiritual challenges including separation, danger, and frequent relocations. Scripture cards provide portable spiritual support that travels with military lifestyles and serves diverse military communities.

"Team Success" Application: Military success creates opportunities with defense contractors, veteran organizations, and military family support networks across multiple installations.

Idea 110: The Veterans Affairs Partnership

"Honoring Service Through Scripture Support"

The Approach: Partner with Veterans Affairs departments and veteran service organizations to provide Scripture cards for veteran counseling, family support, and transition assistance programs.

Why It Works: Veteran services address complex needs including PTSD, disability adjustment, and civilian transition. Scripture cards provide spiritual support that complements professional services for veteran healing and adjustment.

"Team Success" Application: VA success creates opportunities with veteran organizations, disability services, and military transition programs nationwide.

Idea 111: The Police Department Chaplaincy

"Supporting Law Enforcement with Scripture"

The Approach: Partner with police department chaplains and law enforcement support organizations to provide Scripture cards for officer stress management, family support, and community relations.

Why It Works: Law enforcement faces high stress, community tension, and family challenges requiring spiritual support. Scripture cards provide appropriate spiritual resources that serve diverse officer needs and improve community relations.

"Team Success" Application: Police success creates opportunities with law enforcement agencies, public safety organizations, and community policing programs.

Idea 112: The Fire Department Ministry

"Spiritual Support for First Responders"

The Approach: Partner with fire department chaplains and firefighter support organizations to provide Scripture cards for emergency response comfort, trauma support, and family ministry.

Why It Works: Fire service involves life-threatening situations and traumatic experiences requiring spiritual processing and support. Scripture cards provide immediate spiritual comfort for both firefighters and those they serve.

"Team Success" Application: Fire service success creates opportunities with emergency services, trauma counseling, and first responder support networks.

Idea 113: The Government Employee Program

"Faith in Public Service"

The Approach: Partner with government employee associations and public service organizations to provide Scripture cards for workplace encouragement, ethical decision-making support, and professional development.

Why It Works: Government service requires ethical decision-making and public accountability creating needs for spiritual wisdom and encouragement. Scripture cards provide appropriate spiritual support for public servants.

"Team Success" Application: Government success creates opportunities with civil service organizations, public administration programs, and civic leadership institutes.

Idea 114: The Congressional Prayer Program

"Scripture for National Leadership"

The Approach: Partner with Congressional chaplains and legislative prayer groups to provide Scripture cards for political leader encouragement, legislative session support, and bipartisan spiritual connection.

Why It Works: Political leadership requires spiritual wisdom for complex decisions affecting millions. Scripture cards provide non-partisan spiritual resources that serve leaders across political divisions.

"Team Success" Application: Congressional success creates opportunities with political organizations, leadership institutes, and civic engagement programs.

Idea 115: The Judicial System Ministry

"Justice and Scripture in Legal Systems"

The Approach: Partner with court chaplains and legal system ministries to provide Scripture cards for legal professional support, victim services, and justice system spiritual care.

Why It Works: Legal systems deal with human suffering, complex moral issues, and justice administration requiring spiritual wisdom and compassion. Scripture cards provide spiritual resources for legal professionals and those they serve.

"Team Success" Application: Judicial success creates opportunities with legal organizations, victim services, and criminal justice reform programs.

Idea 116: The Diplomatic Corps Support

"Scripture for International Relations"

The Approach: Partner with diplomatic missions and foreign service organizations to provide Scripture cards for diplomatic stress management, cultural bridge-building, and international ministry.

Why It Works: Diplomatic service involves cultural complexity, international tension, and family separation requiring spiritual support and wisdom. Scripture cards provide appropriate spiritual resources for international service.

"Team Success" Application: Diplomatic success creates opportunities with international organizations, cultural exchange programs, and foreign service institutes.

Idea 117: The Intelligence Community Ministry

"Spiritual Strength for National Security"

The Approach: Partner with intelligence community chaplains and security service organizations to provide Scripture cards for high-stress mission support, family encouragement, and spiritual resilience.

Why It Works: Intelligence work involves high stress, security concerns, and moral complexity requiring spiritual strength and guidance. Scripture cards provide appropriate spiritual support for sensitive national security work.

"Team Success" Application: Intelligence success creates opportunities with security agencies, defense contractors, and national security organizations.

Idea 118: The Coast Guard Ministry

"Scripture for Maritime Service"

The Approach: Partner with Coast Guard chaplains and maritime service organizations to provide Scripture cards for sea duty support, rescue mission encouragement, and maritime family ministry.

Why It Works: Maritime service involves isolation, dangerous rescues, and family separation requiring spiritual support and encouragement. Scripture cards provide portable spiritual resources for sea-based ministry.

"Team Success" Application: Coast Guard success creates opportunities with maritime organizations, shipping industry, and ocean ministry programs.

Conclusion

From Simple Sales to Kingdom Transformation: These ideas demonstrate how Scripture cards can become the catalyst for systematic community transformation.

The Team Success Multiplication Effect: Every method creates opportunities for team development, network expansion, and collaborative growth. Individual efforts can become community movements through strategic relationship building and systematic market expansion.

The Ultimate Vision Realized: When communities implement multiple methods simultaneously, the combined impact creates sustainable funding for every ministry need, eliminates financial struggle for every believer, and demonstrates to the world what biblical community can accomplish when unified around mutual success principles.

Your Role in this: Choose the methods that resonate with your personality, skills, and situation. Start with 3-5 approaches, master them completely, then expand systematically. Each successful implementation creates credibility and resources for broader impact.

The "No Need Among Them" Reality: Through these ideas, every Christian community can achieve the Acts 4:32-35 vision where financial need is eliminated through collaborative success, spiritual growth is accelerated through Scripture engagement, and Kingdom impact multiplies through unified effort.

The cards are just the beginning. The ideas are just the tools. The true power lies in transformed communities where your "Team Success" can create mutual prosperity and Kingdom advancement that changes the world.

HERE IS AN INDEX OF THE 100+ IDEA OPPORTUNITIES:

SECTION A: PERSONAL NETWORK FOUNDATIONS

Building Team Success Through Existing Relationships

1. The Family Circle Launch
2. The Church Friends Network
3. The Workplace Connection Strategy
4. The Neighborhood Ambassador Approach
5. The Social Media Friends Circle
6. The Holiday Gift Strategy
7. The Birthday Blessing System
8. The Sympathy and Comfort Ministry
9. The Congratulations Package
10. The Thank You Token Strategy

11. The Encouragement Subscription
12. The Small Group Integration
13. The Teacher and Education Network
14. The Healthcare Heroes Strategy
15. The Senior Saints Strategy
16. The Parent Network Connection
17. The Men's Ministry Connection
18. The Women's Ministry Network
19. The Young Professional Strategy
20. The Community Volunteer Connection

SECTION B: CHURCH AND MINISTRY PARTNERSHIPS

Transforming Congregations into Mutual Success Communities

21. The Sunday School Fundraiser Revolution
22. The Youth Group Mission Trip Engine
23. The Women's Ministry Boutique
24. The Men's Ministry Challenge
25. The VBS Marketplace Ministry
26. The Church Fair Partnership
27. The Pastor Appreciation Strategy
28. The Ministry Leader Network
29. The Retreat Center Partnership
30. The Denominational Conference Circuit
31. The Small Group Supply System
32. The Missions Team Support
33. The Church Plant Partnership
34. The Worship Team Ministry
35. The Children's Ministry Integration

36. The Senior Adult Ministry
37. The College Ministry Connection
38. The Prison Ministry Outreach
39. The Military Ministry Support
40. The Hospital Chaplain Partnership

SECTION C: EVENTS AND SEASONAL STRATEGIES

Maximizing Team Success Through Community Engagement and Timing

41. The Craft Fair Circuit Mastery
42. The Christian Music Festival Network
43. The Homeschool Convention Strategy
44. The Business Networking Breakthrough
45. The Farmers Market Ministry
46. The Wedding Show Partnership
47. The Graduation Gift Campaign
48. The Back-to-School Special
49. The Mother's Day Ministry
50. The Father's Day Focus
51. The Valentine's Ministry
52. The Easter Celebration Strategy
53. The Christmas Market Mastery
54. The Thanksgiving Gratitude Campaign
55. The New Year Resolution Support
56. The Summer Camp Partnership
57. The Community Festival Circuit
58. The Holiday Bazaar Network

59. The Health Fair Ministry
60. The Sports Tournament Ministry

SECTION D: DIGITAL AND ADVANCED STRATEGIES

Leveraging Technology and Innovation for Exponential Team Success

61. The Facebook Marketplace Mastery
62. The Instagram Stories Strategy
63. The YouTube Ministry Channel
64. The Pinterest Inspiration Boards
65. The TikTok Scripture Moments
66. The Email Newsletter Empire
67. The Blog Ministry Platform
68. The Online Christian Forums
69. The Zoom Party Sales
70. The Text Message Marketing
71. The Podcast Sponsorship Strategy
72. The Webinar Workshop Series
73. The Online Marketplace Domination
74. The Affiliate Marketing Network
75. The Digital Product Bundle
76. The Virtual Reality Scripture Experience
77. The Mobile App Integration
78. The AI-Powered Personalization
79. The Blockchain Scripture Registry
80. The Metaverse Ministry Platform

SECTION E: ADVANCED AND CREATIVE STRATEGIES

Revolutionary Approaches for Extraordinary Team Success and Kingdom Impact

81. The Corporate Chaplain Network
82. The Hospital Gift Shop Partnership
83. The Nursing Home Ministry Program
84. The Prison Ministry Transformation
85. The Military Base Outreach
86. The College Campus Ministry
87. The Christian Business Network
88. The Real Estate Closing Gift Program
89. The Medical Office Partnership
90. The Subscription Box Empire
91. The Disaster Relief Ministry
92. The Celebrity Endorsement Strategy
93. The Government Chaplain Network
94. The Entertainment Industry Ministry
95. The Sports Team Ministry
96. The Theme Park Partnership
97. The Cruise Ship Ministry
98. The Space Program Ministry

RETAIL REVOLUTION STRATEGY IDEAS

Transforming Commerce Through Scripture-Based Team Success

99. The Big Box Store Partnership
100. The Specialty Store Network

101. The Online Marketplace Domination *(duplicate of #73)*
102. The Subscription Box Integration *(duplicate of #90)*
103. The Pop-up Shop Strategy
104. The Corporate Gift Program
105. The Retail Training Institute
106. The Wholesale Distribution Network
107. The Retail Technology Integration
108. The International Retail Expansion

GOVERNMENT AND MILITARY IDEAS

Serving Those Who Serve Through Scripture-Based Team Success

109. The Military Base Ministry Network *(duplicate of #85)*
110. The Veterans Affairs Partnership
111. The Police Department Chaplaincy
112. The Fire Department Ministry
113. The Government Employee Program
114. The Congressional Prayer Program
115. The Judicial System Ministry
116. The Diplomatic Corps Support
117. The Intelligence Community Ministry
118. The Coast Guard Ministry

Books By the *Team Success Network* - In The "Team Success" Series:

Book 1 - Kingdom of Heaven – Team Success Network

Book 2 - Building Duplicatable "Mutual Success Team" Business Projects

Book 3 - Team Success Network: Leadership, Development, Summits, & Discipleship

Book 4 - AI Tools - Team Success Network - Enhancing Mutual Success Teams Using AI Tools

Book 5 - Team Success Network: Global Organization & Resources

Book 6 - 200+ Business Project Ideas – For Mutual Success Teams

Book 7 - The FAITH HEALING TRAININGS - Learn Healing As a Skill

Book 8 - Using Christian Decks as Your First "Mutual Success Project"

Meet the Author – Elijah Jonathon Stone

Founder of the Team Success Network

Hi, I'm Elijah. I wrote this book because I believe God is calling the Church into a new era—where we don't just gather, we build. I'm not a celebrity, a pastor of a mega church, or a spiritual expert. I'm someone like you—who saw the need and heard the call.

The Team Success Network is not just a concept. It's a movement of real believers working together to bring God's Kingdom into real life—through unity, purpose, and mutual success. I hope this book encourages and equips you to step into your role.

If this vision speaks to your heart, I'd love to hear from you.

Email me personally: elijah@teamsuccessnetwork.com

Let's keep building—together.

Stay Connected – Your Next Step Starts Now

You've made it through this book—but that doesn't mean the journey is over. In fact, it may just be beginning.

The Team Success Network was created for people like you—believers who are ready to live differently, work together, and take action that transforms lives. If something in these pages sparked a new idea, birthed a desire to join or lead a team, or helped you experience a breakthrough—we want to know. Your story matters.

Let's move from inspiration to action.

Reach out to us:

📩 To Connect – connect@teamsuccessnetwork.com

📩 Share What God Is Doing – results@teamsuccessnetwork.com

📩 Send Us Documents or Team Reports – docs@teamsuccessnetwork.com

📩 Write Elijah Personally – elijah@teamsuccessnetwork.com

You're not alone in this. The Kingdom is advancing—and we're building it together. Let's keep going.